PROTESTANT PATRIARCH

PROTESTANT PATRIARCH

THE LIFE OF

CYRIL LUCARIS

(1572-1638)

PATRIARCH OF
CONSTANTINOPLE

GEORGE A. HADJIANTONIOU

JOHN KNOX PRESS
RICHMOND, VIRGINIA

Library of Congress Catalog Card Number: 61-7594

FOREWORD

For the past fifteen hundred years, the Latin and Greek traditions in the community of Christians have had disparate histories, with widely contrasting experiences to separate and to complicate their relations. The formal schism between Rome and Constantinople (now approaching its millenium) is only an outward sign of the deeper schism in the soul of Christendom. Since the seventh century, Byzantine Christianity had to exist first as the state of a beleaguered fortress-Empire and then as the religion of a persecuted minority under the Crescent scimitar. It bears the scars of the ruin it suffered at the hands of Crusaders and Turks alike. For ten centuries it survived without the kind of academic institutions which helped raise the West from barbarism. It lived more by its liturgy than its literature, more by the *lex orandi, lex credendi* than by the genius of its doctors.

Small wonder, then, that the images of Eastern Christianity in Western manuals of church history are usually uncomprehending—with their phrases about "theological stagnation," "arrested development," "traditionalism." Small wonder, too, that the sporadic efforts at *rapprochement* between East and West have been so volatile—and so unfamiliar to the generality of Western Christians. Now that the modern ecumenical movement has put Orthodox and Protestant theologians back into dialogue, this ignorance of ours about their history is worse than embarrassing. It turns our conversation into cross-talk.

One of the most noteworthy chapters in this strange history has to do with the century-long, backstage parley that went on between various Protestants and Greeks in the sixteenth and seventeenth centuries. Many Protestants, uneasy about their breach with the Christian past, saw in Orthodoxy a sounder link than Rome with the church catholic. At least a few Orthodox leaders saw in Protestantism not only an authentic reformatory impulse but also an ally against the aggressions of Counter-Reformation Rome. The most dramatic episode in this chapter was the brief flowering of Cyril Lucaris, Ecumenical Patriarch of Constantinople (1620-1638, intermittently), educator, statesman, Calvinist theologian!

5

It is, therefore, a gracious act of Dr. Hadjiantoniou's that he offers us a partial redemption from our culpable ignorance about this particular intersection of our separate histories, East and West, which meet in Cyril. He has rescued a great man from undeserved oblivion; he has illuminated a whole generation of European history from a new angle; he reads well! One has only to check the entry, Cyril Lucar, in the *Oxford Dictionary of the Christian Church* to see the blurred snapshots of Cyril presently mounted in a scanty literature. *Protestant Patriarch* gives us a full-length portrait. It is an admiring portrait, drawn by a man who is a friend to Cyril's friends and a foe to Cyril's foes. It is a study that will repay careful inspection.

Naturally, every reader brings his own concerns to a biography. My own found their focus in Chapter 11—plus the Appendix. Here we have a detailed study of the most important theological event in Cyril's career: his famous *Confessio Fidei*. In the Appendix there is an English translation of the *Confessio*—the only published version I know of since the 17th century. This Confession, or Catechism, is one of those things more often mentioned than actually read and studied. Now it can be examined at first hand. It is, quite literally, a *phenomenon:* an official doctrinal statement published in and for the Orthodox church—militantly Calvinistic! It *had* to be repudiated by the other Orthodox leaders—and it was. But in the course of the controversy, here fully discussed, we are provided with some vivid sidelights on the murky problem of the respective roles of literary and liturgical forms in the transit of Christian faith and order through history.

The reader will discover in its opening pages that this is a partisan book, replete with unblemished heroes and unmitigated villains. Cyril —and his Protestant allies—are the heroes. The Romans—and their Turkish dupes—are the villains. One cannot deny that there is a substantial core of truth in this. By any account, Cyril stands on higher ground than the unholy alliance of Catholics and Turks that did him in. Nevertheless, historical events are rarely univalent and a historian might rightly be expected to realize the anomalies and unrealities of Cyril's situation. Dr. Hadjiantoniou supplies much of the data needed for a critical evaluation. His own is unreservedly protestant.

This book opens a wide window on a hitherto blocked view of a momentous affair. It provides ample clues for further exploration. It affords a basic reference for Protestants who would like to become knowledgeable in Orthodox history. One wishes for it the wide— and critical—reading it deserves.

Albert C. Outler

CONTENTS

▣ CHAPTER I

EARLY YEARS

H E WAS ONLY A BOY OF TWELVE when in 1584 he arrived in Venice,[1] and that was the first time he had gone so far away from home. He had spent many days and many nights on the ship before he saw the City of the Lagoons rising suddenly from the sea before his eyes, as if by magic. And what a world that was into which he had stepped! What a contrast to the poor, homely environment of his own little town in far-off Crete, with its winding cobbled lanes, its humble houses, its gardens and orchards, and an occasional stray goat finding its way into the streets. How different was the great, noisy city, with its stately buildings, its big squares, and its watery lanes.

Little Constantine Lucaris probably lodged either at the "Salvatico" or the "Leon Bianco," or at some other of the famous and flourishing hotels of the city. For, at a time when travel in Italy was a rather risky affair for foreigners who happened to hold religious views other than those approved by Rome, Venice had flung her gates open, and a continuous stream of travelers came in and out of her canals. But Lucaris did not stay long at the hotel, for almost at the same time another Greek came to Venice, a man quite famous in his time, who took the little Cretan boy under his protection. Maximos Margunios had already been consecrated as bishop of the island of Cythera, off the southern coast of Greece, but the Venetian authorities of the island, for some reason of their own, would not permit him to land there and exercise the duties of his office.[2] So Margunios betook himself to Venice, which was already well known to him from the years of his youth, when he had succeeded in spending the whole of a considerable paternal inheritance in his vain effort to set up a

9

Greek printing house in that city. It was here, therefore, that he came to stay until such a time as permission would be granted to him to go and settle in his island See. And it was fortunate for young Constantine Lucaris that he arrived at Venice at the time of Margunios' self-exile there, for though Margunios had a few strange ideas, which had at times landed him into trouble and on one occasion brought him within sight of a Roman prison, he was an excellent man—a man of upright character and great culture. He was something of a poet, too—his *Anacreontian Hymns* having attained the distinction of repeated editions.[3] Judging from his letters, which are written in a style of irreproachable classical correctness, we gather that he was a classic scholar. But besides a cultured mind, old Margunios had a warm heart, which at times would break through the hedges of classical correctness and forget itself in the more homely "demotic" idiom. And so we see in one of his letters to his young protégé that he departed so far from his classical standards as to actually call him "My lad Constantine."[4] Such a grievous lapse, however, could only occur in connection with one whom he loved dearly, for we know that he had conceived a strong affection for that compatriot of his— for he, too, hailed from Crete.

It was by this man that Constantine was taught his Greek, his Latin, and his Italian, and it was under him that he took his first steps in philosophy. It is touching to see, in the letters exchanged between teacher and pupil on their occasional partings, the paternal care with which the old man followed the studies of the boy, and the pride which he felt over his progress. In one of these letters he commends his pupil for the beautiful expressions he had used in one of his own, and although he is obliged to remark that unfortunately the handwriting was not equally beautiful, he expresses the hope that since the greater gift was given him, the lesser one would follow in time.[5] But judging from Lucaris' manuscripts which have come down to us, this hope of his old teacher seems to have remained unfulfilled. Margunios' love for his pupil was returned in rich measure. Constantine came to love him as a second father, and this love seems to have been the recognition of something greater than the teaching of Latin and Greek, for Margunios somewhere calls the young boy his "son in Christ."[6] At any rate, the influence which the teacher exercised on the mind of the pupil was great and manifold. In more than one respect he had become the ideal which the young boy aimed to copy. Constantine even affected the peculiar style of his teacher, for after he had parted with Margunios one of his friends writes to tell him that he detected a "Margunizing" tendency in his letters.[7] And so it was through Margunios' window that Constantine had his first glimpse of Venice.

If Lucaris had hoped to see Venice in the height of her glory, he had arrived about a hundred years too late. Gone were the days when the Republic was the clearinghouse of the world. Gone were the days when six commercial fleets with their corresponding caravans were equipped and manned every year and dispatched as far as Russia, Siam, and India in the East, and as far as Spain and the British Isles in the West. The three hundred odd cargo boats, of which these fleets were composed, had carried proudly the flag of St. Mark on all the sea lanes to bring to Venice the merchandise of distant countries. And so long as the Republic's hand held firmly the monopoly of the world's commerce, the riches which flooded her were fabulous. To all this, however, a young Portuguese sailor had long since put an end. The year 1497 saw Vasco da Gama rounding the Cape of Good Hope, and a new route—a water passage—to the Indies and the East was discovered, a route which would dispose of caravans and all the resulting inconveniences, such as the heavy taxes levied by the cities which lay in their route, or the costly delays caused by the transfer of cargo from ship to caravan and vice versa. It was not long before this new waterway became popular, and Venice found herself suddenly outside the routes which commerce began to follow. Priuli records in his "Chronicle" what a heavy blow it was for the Venetians when the news of the new discovery reached their city. "When this news reached Venice, the whole city felt it greatly, and remained stupefied, and the wisest held it as the worst news which could ever come."[8]

But, although young Constantine missed the zenith, he saw a beautiful sunset. In the lands of the Mediterranean the name of Venice was still great and the legend of her riches still alive. Long after Lucaris' day, many a young Greek mother sang her little one to sleep by reassuring her that she had ordered

"... in Venice her wardrobe,
And her jewelry."

The day of the great Republic was not yet over, and its closing
hours were worthy of their glorious past. Constantine undoubtedly
witnessed on Ascension Day that beautiful ceremony of the
"Espousals" of the Doge with the Sea. An English writer who
happened to visit Venice shortly after Lucaris had been there, has
left us a description of that remarkable rite.[9] The *Bucentaur*, a
triumphal galley, richly gilt, brought the Doge with the *clarissi-
moes* of the Signiory out into the open, with every available boat
in Venice following in its train. When the galley reached a certain
point, the Doge with all solemnity threw into the sea a ring—the
nuptial pledge of the sea's subjection to Venice. This custom had
its origin in the days of Pope Alexander III and was scrupulously
observed long after it had lost its meaning. In recognition of the
services which the Venetian fleet had rendered him, the Pope had
offered the Doge a golden ring, and commanded him to cast it
into the sea. "This ceremony," he told him, "shall on this day be
yearly observed both by thee and by thy successors, that posterity
may know how you have purchased the dominion of the sea by
your valour, and made it subject unto thee, as a wife to her
husband." The marital fidelity, alas, had long ago been sadly
broken, but the mystical ring was yearly cast into the sea with
all the pomp and splendor of the former glorious days.

In a way Lucaris was fortunate to have come to Venice in the
days of her decline, for it was then that her beauty reached its
maturity.[10] The less her income grew, the more lavishly did she
spend it on her palaces, her churches, and her pageants. As the
little Cretan boy wandered in this great city, he must have stopped
before many a beautiful house front, decorated by a Titian, a
Tintoretto, or a Veronese. He entered the stately churches and
stood with admiration before their mosaics. He walked to the
Piazza di Rialto, and saw important-looking patricians walking
under the famous colonnade, discussing politics. He saw women
dressed in silks and velvets, covered with precious stones, and
tottering on their richly ornamented *zoccoli*, those strange clogs
with extremely high heels which obliged their wearers to lean on

the shoulders of their servants, lest they fall. He saw the city, half-asleep in daytime, suddenly waking up in the evening for another night of revelry. He listened to her laughter and her song. "They sang in the squares, in the streets, on the canals; the shop-keepers sang as they sold their wares; the workmen sang as they left their work; the gondolier sang while he waited for his master." In addition to all this he also saw the great immorality of the city. That was by no means a period of high moral standards, espe-cially in Italy; yet many an Italian town would have been shocked by the excesses of Venice. How different all this—the noisy streets and the cheerful canals—from the dear little town which the young boy had left behind!

There was another sense in which Lucaris had arrived in Venice too late—and that was of even greater importance to him. When roaming about the city and going by the Piazzetta near the Grand Canal, he must have come across the great library where the valuable collection of Greek manuscripts, bequeathed to the city by the Greek Cardinal Bessarion, was kept. And he would be shown the building nearby where the press of Aldus Manutius used to print Greek classics in fine editions, and where the famous Aldine Academy used to meet. All this was a reminder that in the not very distant past Venice had been an outstanding center of Hellenic studies. But now that, too, was more or less a matter of the past. The century which was now drawing to its close had witnessed great changes. It had been an era of dis-coveries and inventions, which had opened before the human mind horizons far wider than it had ever known. Consequently people were no longer content to take their knowledge second-hand from the Greeks and the Latins. Thus the century which had opened with a flourishing of the classical studies, was now witnessing at its close a rapid decline of these studies.

However, this past was not too distant to make an impression on young Lucaris. Men like George of Trebizond, who not so very long before had been teaching Greek in Venice; or the two Apostolios, father and son, who had linked their names with the first Greek editions in that city; or John Lascaris, that cultured ambassador of the King of France in Venice, who had opened his rich library to the scholars of that city; or the Cretan Demetrios

Ducas, who had supervised a good many Venetian editions of Greek books before proceeding to Alcala in Spain to assist the Cardinal Ximenes in the publication of the first Polyglot Bible; or Demetrios Zenos, who had come from Zante to devote himself to the translation of the classics, and was later entrusted by Francis I of France with the education of his son Henry; or Contoleon the copyist; or the other two Cretans, Zacharias Callierghis and Nicholas Blastos, who had contributed, the former his work and the latter his money, to found a Greek printing house in Venice, thus enriching the world of books with some beautiful editions; and above all the great Mark Mussuros, that wise and learned man, yet another son of Crete, who proved to be Aldus' right hand in his valuable editions of the Greek classics, and who, as Aldus puts it, had made Venice "a second Athens"[11] before proceeding to Padua to occupy the chair of Greek there—men like these are not easily forgotten, and Constantine must have been very proud going about in a city so full of such memories. It was not more than ten years since Theotokopoulos had completed his studies under Titian and had left Venice for Spain, to win for himself, under the name of "El Greco," a place among the world's great painters.

Even Aldus himself, although an Italian, was at heart a Greek. On the flyleaf of the volume of Aristotle which was in his hands while yet in Crete, Lucaris must have noticed the small phrase, "This book was printed in Venice, in the house of Aldus Manutius, a Roman and a Lover of Greece." It is doubtful whether Greece ever had a lover more ardent and more noble than Aldus. His printing house was itself a little Greek colony. From his instructions to the workmen which have been preserved for us, and which are all in Greek, we infer that the majority of these workmen were Greeks, a large number of them from the island of Crete. And the same is true of the other printing house in Venice, the one founded by Blastos and Callierghis, a fact which inspired Mark Mussuros to compose that delightful little poem which we find at the beginning of his *Etymologicum Magnum*:

> "But why should I wonder at the spirit of the
> Cretans, for it was Minerva herself, who, at the

command of her father, instructed them in the beauties of art! It was a Cretan who chiselled the stamp; a Cretan who stringed together the pieces of brass; a Cretan who pricked them; a Cretan who melted the lead. A Cretan met the expense, and it is a Cretan who is writing these verses . . ."[12]

But to come back to Aldus, the Academy which he founded was no lesser evidence of his love for Greece than his printing house. In fact, the Academy was born in the printing house. It was composed of the scholars whom Aldus had gathered around him to help with the preparation of his editions. Some of these were so enthusiastic over their new Greek studies that they even Hellenized their Italian names. Thus the Secretary of the Academy, scholar Fortiguerra, became Carteromachus. The love of these men for the Greek language was so great that the statutory law of the Academy, which was written in Greek, imposed on its members the obligation to use only the Greek language in their conversation with each other.[13] And a fine had to be paid for every infraction of this rule. The money thus collected was kept in a box which was opened at a given time, and if the sum contained proved sufficient, Aldus would treat the members of the Academy to a good dinner, "a grand one, and not one fit only for printers." Unfortunately the annals of the Academy do not mention how many such dinners the academicians enjoyed.

All this, however, was now a matter of the past. Aldus died, and not long after both the printing house and the Academy were buried with him. The other printing house, founded by Blastos and Callierghis, had been obliged by the hard times which followed the League of Cambrai to move to Rome, where thanks to the encouragement received from Pope Leo X it survived for a little longer. So, as far as Venice was concerned, all that noble Greek activity was ended, and if young Constantine sometimes felt the longing to hear the sound of his native tongue outside his own house, he either had to go for a haircut, as most barbers at that time in Venice were Greeks (their shops being among the most popular centers of local gossip), or else to search for one of

the shops where the famous Greek wine, so popular to the Venetians of that time, was for sale. A rather far cry from the times of
Aldus and Mussuros!

Aldus passed away, but not before he had established a tradition, and this tradition was to reassert itself in Lucaris' career in
later days. On more than one occasion Aldus and his books proved
to be a stumbling block to the good relations between Rome and
Venice. Venice was very proud of her extensive trade in books,
while Rome was not very enthusiastic. The authorities of the
"Index" had again and again tried to interfere and place the
products of the Venetian press on the prohibited lists.[14] And this
only served to increase the friction which already existed between
Venice and Rome. The Venetians had always been commercial-
minded. And even though they claimed to be good Catholics, they
were very careful not to permit the demands of the Church to
override their commercial interests. They were fond of saying:
"Siamo Veneziani, poi Christiani." ("We are first of all Venetians,
and then Christians.")[15] And all through their history they held
themselves true to that maxim. So at a time when the bonfires of
the Inquisition were claiming their victims by the hundreds in
other countries of Europe, Venice resisted the establishment of
the Holy Office on her soil. She was too good a merchant not to
realize that personal security and security of one's property were
indispensable for commercial enterprise, and thus she avoided
making the same mistake as Spain, who let herself be bled white
by the Inquisitors. When finally Venice was obliged to admit that
institution into her territory, she placed it under strict civic control, so that it became quite innocuous. The archives of the Venetian Holy Office mention only six cases of people who were put to
death for their religious convictions.[16] Thus St. Mark kept St.
Peter at a safe distance, and the result was that there reigned in
Venice freedom of thought and a spirit of independence which
were undreamt-of at that time in any other city of Italy. As someone has put it, "Freedom of thought was at that time a refugee
in Venice."[17] It was in that city of freedom that young Lucaris
spent the first formative years of his youth. And we may not be
far wrong if we trace the origin of the proud spirit of independ-

ence which he exhibited all through his life, and his deep antip-
athy against the papal claims of authority, to the early influence
of the freedom-loving Republic of the Lagoons.

It is doubtful whether Lucaris got anything more out of Venice
—apart from his Greek and Latin and his sense of personal independence—which was to stand him in such good stead in years
to come. Venice was one of the most important centers in Italy,
in which the Reformed doctrines were cultivated within the
Roman Church itself. An active branch of the "Oratory of Divine
Love" was operating in that city. That famous book on "The
benefits bestowed by Christ," which though written by a devout
Catholic was publicly burned in Rome, had circulated widely in
Venice; and the doctrine of justification by faith had been taught
there by a number of otherwise loyal children of the Church.
Although this movement belongs to a time prior to that of the
arrival of Lucaris in Venice, it is possible that it had not died out
completely, and that in this city he heard for the first time the
teaching of those doctrines which he was to adopt and defend in
later years. We find no trace, however, of such a possibility in his
letters. If young Constantine heard of those doctrines in Venice,
he either rejected them completely or else, finding them too deep
for him, ignored them. It is more likely that his first real acquaintance with the Reformed faith may be traced to a later time. For
the time being he is quite content with lesser things—Latin and
Greek. His old dream of being a scholar is now at last being fulfilled, and he asks for nothing better. His cup is running over.

CHAPTER 2

BACK IN CRETE

B UT THE DREAM CAME SUDDENLY TO AN END. Probably financial
difficulties had forced his parents to call him back at the
end of four years. Anyway, it was with a heavy heart that
Constantine bade farewell to his beloved Venice and to his old
teacher and set sail for his native island. But in spite of his sorrow
at leaving Venice behind, his heart could not but give a leap of
joy at the first distant sight of the familiar outline of the snow-
capped Psiloritis, the famous Ida of the ancients,

> "In pitch rich above other,
> Of oaks the pregnant mother."

Thomas Dallam, an English traveler who sailed by this island
a short time later bearing a present from Queen Elizabeth to the
Sultan in Constantinople, records in his diary that he was told by
a fellow passenger, a Jew, that on the top of the high mountain
stood the bronze figure of a man who held a bow bent as if he
were shooting toward the East.[1] The story of that Jewish passenger was very probably some folk tale of that time which orig-
inated from the ancient Greek story of the bronze giant Talus,
son of Vulcan, who walked thrice daily round the whole island
keeping watch over its coasts. But whatever its origin, the story
was a true symbol of the spirit of the Cretan people of that time.
In those sad years following the fall of Constantinople, when
Greece seemed to have gone to sleep and its history was a sad
record of intellectual and moral decline, a small flame of the
Hellenic spirit was kept alive in Crete. It has been well said that

at that time Crete was the "Little Hellas." Like another Talus she
was keeping her vigil, waiting patiently for the dawn.

At that time Crete was a Venetian colony. She had been one
for nearly four hundred years, and the Venetians had found it by
no means an easy colony to hold. The first one hundred and fifty
years of Venetian occupation were marked by an obstinate, if
unequal, struggle of the hardy Greek islanders against the proud
Mistress of the Seas. That stubborn struggle of the Cretans, which
was in such sharp contrast to the passive resignation with which
the rest of Greece had accepted her fate, was something that the
Venetians could not understand; and they tried to explain it by
attributing to the Cretans a double dose of original sin. However,
the fact remains that the Hellenic spirit of freedom survived on
the mountains of Crete longer than in any other part of Greece.[2]
And even when the Cretans, utterly exhausted, were forced to
calm down, it was only after they had to some extent conquered
their conquerors. Like the Roman conquerors of Greece, the
Venetian masters of Crete were allowed a peaceful enjoyment of
their conquest only after they had been Hellenized to a considerable degree. In the countryside the Venetians were completely
absorbed by the Greeks. There the Venetian colonists adopted the
Greek language, the Greek customs, and even the Greek religion;
their only link with the past being their sonorous names, such as
Dandolos, Cornaros, Venieris. One very rarely saw a Latin monk
or priest in the countryside. In the cities, however, the Venetian
element managed to hold its own; and it was there that the
bishops of the ten Sees of the island had sought refuge, together
with a host of priests and monks of the Franciscan, Dominican,
and Augustinian orders who did not dare go out to the villages
in order to fulfill their mission.[3]

But the spirit of freedom is as a rule a costly thing, and the
statistics concerning the population of the island at that time bear
witness to this. At the time of the Venetian occupation of Crete
its population amounted to five or six hundred thousand,[4] but
when young Lucaris returned home it had been reduced to a
little more than one hundred and seventy thousand. The social,
intellectual, and religious condition of the people was not good
either. The majority of the numerous priests and monks were

illiterate, or very nearly so, and in the case of most, superstition and ignorance had replaced spiritual religion.[5] The few existing schools on the island could offer hardly more than the mere reading of ecclesiastical books. There was, however, one bright exception. And that was the Monastery of St. Catherine in the town of Candia. A school operating within the walls of this monastery offered to its pupils an education of a much higher standard. And thanks to the services of the good monk Meletios Blastos, many a young Cretan had gone out into the world with the thirst for something higher.[6] One of these was young Constantine Lucaris.

Blastos was famous in his time and had made quite a name for himself. Nearly a century after his death, when Crete had already been captured by the Turks, there was printed in Venice a poem by a certain Marinos Tzanes, in which the poet laments the loss of his native island.[7] In this rather odd poem, the two chief towns of the island, Candia and Rethimno, are pictured as quarreling with each other over which was superior. At last Rethimno deals a deadly blow at her opponent by pointing out that if Candia shone at all it was by the light which she had borrowed from Rethimno. And one of the luminaries which Candia had borrowed from Rethimno was "the good Meletios Blastos, the great teacher." It was at the feet of this monk that Constantine had sat for his first lessons. And in the years which followed he never forgot his teacher. Even when the Church had called him to its highest offices, he always found time to send a brief note to the old monk in Crete. On one occasion he writes, "How you have gladdened my heart with your letter!"[8] And on another, when he had been facing great difficulties in the Church of Alexandria, he says, "I was passing through a great storm when your letter came and brought me great comfort."[9] "Let others lisp childish talk," writes the celebrated pupil to his teacher in the same letter, "let others play with childish toys; I know thee only as the well of Solomon's wisdom which offers its waters in abundance to all who are thirsty."

Apart from our knowledge about his first teacher, we know very little of Lucaris' earliest days in Crete. About his parents we know almost nothing. In later days, speaking of them, he says, "Not of a mixed stock, barbarians, hybrid, slaves, unknown, were my parents, but Greeks, respectable, free, prominent both in the State and in the Church."[10] And his good friend Meletios Pegas, Patriarch of Alexandria, desiring to instill into the heart of the young boy a desire for great things, wrote to him, "To belong to great parents, is not the work of chance—it is God's gift."[11] Beyond this, however, and the fact that his father's name was Stephanos, our information about Lucaris' parents is very scanty. According to Nicolaos Comnenos Papadopolus, Stephanos Lucaris' family hailed from the Dalmatian coast, and was of noble descent, being related to the imperial house of the Palaeologi.[12] However, Stephanos and his family passed through hard times, and were at last reduced to extreme poverty. They were obliged to leave their country residence and settle in Candia, where old Lucaris took up the job of a butcher, his wife took in occasional washing, and little Constantine was apprenticed to a fisherman. It was on a trip to Alexandria, on the fisherman's boat, that he became acquainted with his distant relative Meletios Pegas, who thereafter took him under his protection and was largely responsible for his being sent to the West for higher studies. It is difficult to say whether this romantic story is true, as our only authority for it, Papadopolus, is not always trustworthy in his stories.

However, although young Constantine, now in his sixteenth year, had his dream of learning so suddenly interrupted, he did not resign himself to his fate. If Venice was for the time being beyond his grasp, he could still do something in his present environment. So he unearthed a number of books which his old teacher Margunios had left somewhere in Candia, and in the company of the *Opuscules* of Plutarch, a book or two of Cicero, the orations of Demosthenes, the logic of Flaminius, a book of Aristotle, one or two volumes of Eusebius, and a Latin dictionary, he had anything but a lazy time in his father's home.[13]

His heart, however, was still in Venice. His one desire was to go back and resume his studies. And every courier leaving Crete for Venice was sure to carry a letter from Constantine to Margunios, in which he strongly implored his old friend to take him back to Venice and give him another chance to finish his studies there.[14]

CHAPTER 3

A STUDENT IN PADUA

A<small>T LAST CONSTANTINE'S PERSEVERANCE WAS REWARDED.</small> But how did this change come about? Did old Stephanos come into some unexpected money, which enabled him to send his son back to Italy? Or was it Margunios who kept the promise he had made to his young friend that he would help him continue his studies with all the means at his disposal, even if that meant that he would have to share with him his scanty meals?[1] Or was it his newly discovered relative, the Patriarch of Alexandria, who paid the expenses of a university course for his young protégé? We cannot say, but what matters is that in a few months' time, a year at the most, the Cretan interlude came to an end, and in 1589 we find Lucaris back in Italy—not in Venice this time, but in Padua. This means that the period of his private education under Margunios was over, and he was now considered sufficiently prepared to be launched into a real university course. It was not before another six years, after he had graduated at Padua, that he left Italy for good.

Padua had one of the oldest and best known universities in Europe, and it was at the height of its glory when Lucaris enrolled in it. It was about the same time that Galileo was appointed to the chair of mathematics. The students were enrolled according to their nationality, and they thus formed the various "nations" of the University. Each nation chose one or two representatives—*conciliarii*—and these, together with the Rectors, composed the governing body of the University. At the time of Lucaris' arrival the "nations" in Padua were very numerous, as students from all parts of Europe who wanted to specialize in some particular field of their academic studies, especially those studying medicine or law, did not fail to put in some time of study in Padua. Lucaris just missed by a year or two William Harvey, that renowned discoverer of the circulation of the blood, who was drawn to Padua by the fame of Fabricius, the great anatomist.

Unfortunately we do not have much information about the members of the Greek "nation" at the time when Lucaris was there. We know that there was an endowment for Cypriot students, and so we find the names of a number of young men from Cyprus on the lists of the Paduan alumni.[2] There were also a good number from Crete, as well as from other islands and the mainland of Greece. We find at least one distinguished name among the Greek fellow students of Lucaris, that of Ioannes Sozomenos, who later became the librarian of St. Mark's Library in Venice.[3] Curiously enough, this man is also connected with the Scottish "nation," as he was elected a *conciliarius* for this "nation" in 1589 or 1590. That was, however, by no means the only case, for in the forty or so years that preceded Lucaris' arrival in Padua we find at least two other Greeks, who were given the honor of being *conciliarii* of the Scottish "nation," and three more who acted in that capacity for the English one.[4]

Of the various Greeks who occupied chairs in Padua, probably no one was more famous than Mark Mussuros. Erasmus, who was among his students, speaks of the great numbers who were drawn to his lectures and mentions the case of Raphael Regio, the seventy-year-old professor at that university, who braved bitter cold in order to attend the early morning classes of Mussuros.[5]

Two of the professors whose lectures Lucaris attended are well known to us. Both were professors of philosophy—Francis Piccolomini[6] and Caesar Cremonini,[7] and both have left their mark in the history of the University. The first was already an elderly man and approaching the close of his remarkable career when young Lucaris joined his classes. He was a man of vast learning and held many responsible offices besides his professorial chair. The younger man, Cremonini, was called to the second chair of philosophy when Lucaris was in his second year. A sketch of Cremonini, made by a contemporary of his, pictures him as a big, tall man with a high forehead and searching eyes. Cremonini soon

became very popular among the students at Padua, not only because of his fluent style and well-prepared lectures, but also
because of his habit of gathering his students around him and
discussing with them the subject on which he had been lecturing
in the classroom. An incident during Lucaris' third year gives us
some idea of the spirit which prevailed in the University of
Padua. A deputation from the University, with Cremonini and
Piccolomini as its leaders, presented itself before the Senate of
Venice, and secured a decree by which a ban was imposed on the
Jesuit Fathers as teachers in the University. They were forbidden
to lecture within the University grounds on any other subject
except that of *literae humaniores*.[8] That such a measure against
the Church's most powerful Order should be sought after and
secured by men who were otherwise considered to be this church's
faithful sons is a sufficient indication of the liberal spirit which
prevailed in the University. It should be noted that it would have
been impossible for such a measure to be taken in any other
university in Italy. Padua was, in reality, the University of Venice,
as that city had no university of its own, and to use Renan's
phrase, Padua was the "Quartier Latin" of Venice.[9] It is not surprising, therefore, that much of its teaching was characterized
by a distinct divergence from the doctrines of Rome. Indeed, the
Holy See did not pretend to conceal its great displeasure at the
freedom of thought which the students were permitted and at
the very limited interference in University affairs which the
Bishop of Padua was allowed. This displeasure, however, made
hardly any impression on the Venetian authorities. So the University of Padua continued for a long time to be the most important center of liberal thought in southern Europe, and to attract
an increasing number of students from Britain, Germany, and
other Protestant countries—students who would not feel themselves safe in attending the other Italian universities.

It was in that cosmopolitan and congenial environment that
young Lucaris spent six whole years working for his degree. The
progress of his studies during these years was by no means
smooth. As a matter of fact, this warmhearted Cretan youth gave
some anxious times to his old friend Margunios in Venice. At one
time the rumor came to the ears of Margunios that his young

protégé had, for some reason of his own, stopped attending the public instruction at the University, preferring to have private tutors. So Margunios was obliged to write to him a severe letter, which seems to have been effective in driving this wild idea from the young man's head.[10] But even more serious trouble followed. Some fifty years before Lucaris' time a number of foreign students had put in a petition to carry arms. It seems that the necessary permits had been granted to a number of English and other students.[11] And now after so long, this petition of the foreign students was unearthed in the archives of Venice and the craze for carrying arms revived. We can imagine the astonishment of old Margunios when the news reached him that his young protégé had been seen strolling about the streets of Padua with a beautiful gilt sword hanging gracefully from his waist. And this at a time when he ought to be keeping to his room and making the most of every minute of daylight, since he, like most students in Padua, could hardly afford the luxury of a small oil lamp. It is not surprising, therefore, that shortly after this Lucaris received another letter, in the well-known strict classical style, in which his old teacher told him in very plain language what he thought of his foolish behavior.[12]

Except, however, for these two incidents, it does not seem that Margunios had ever again the occasion to feel the least anxiety about his protégé's progress in his university course. And it is touching to see how the old man himself enjoyed that course through his correspondence with his young friend. For, with the exception of one letter in which he informed Lucaris that he was suffering from an attack of erysipelas, and asked him to inquire of the "doctors" at Padua and send him some medicine,[13] most of their correspondence consisted of exercises which the older man set to the younger one on the differences between the philosophy of Plato and that of Aristotle, or on other similar subjects.[14]

But even though Lucaris was obliged in deference to his old teacher to abandon very reluctantly his beautiful sword, he did not miss any opportunity for giving expression to the overflow of energy and mirth which were bubbling over in his youthful Cretan heart. At least three times in the course of his studies he must have taken part in the boisterous ceremony of the installation of the new Rector of the University, and been entertained together with the other students at a banquet given by that dignitary, or, in the case of a particularly stingy Rector, he would have been offered at least wine and tidbits. And then he must have gone along with the others to participate in the wild ceremony of tearing to pieces the clothes of the new Rector and obliging him to redeem any rags which Lucaris had snatched, at a price which would keep him in pocket money for some time. And he certainly never missed any of the other festivities with which the Paduan students tried to enliven their otherwise hard and extremely frugal life.[15]

At last the long years of study came to an end. The terror-inspiring private examination was over, and had been followed by the less intimidating public test. And then the great day arrived when, in the presence of professors, fellow students, and friends, Lucaris was acclaimed in the cathedral a *laureatus* of the University of Padua. Thus his long dream had come to a beautiful end, and suddenly Lucaris felt himself "grown-up." Gone were the days of carefree youth. Now he was a man of twenty-three, and feeling the need for action. The student days were good, but now something bigger was stirring in his heart. The call of his enslaved people came to his ears. A letter from his great patron, good old Meletios Pegas, the Patriarch of Alexandria, came as a reminder of his duty toward his suffering motherland and set him thinking along these lines: ". . . Labours and hardships are in store for thee, but the crown will certainly follow . . . Do not get weary in the good fight. Show thyself worthy of God who hath enlisted thee in His army. Refresh my bowels in the Lord. Let me not be disappointed in the great hopes I have for thee."[16]

It was thus in a sober and thoughtful frame of mind that Constantine bade farewell to Italy and all the good things life had given him there, and turned his face toward the East and the work which was now calling him.

🔳 CHAPTER 4

MISSION TO POLAND

IN OCTOBER 1596 TWO GREEK CLERGYMEN, the Rev. Nicephorus Cantacuzinos and the Rev. Cyril Lucaris, entered the little Polish town of Brest, better known in recent times as Brest-Litovsk. The second of the above two was none other than the young graduate of the University of Padua, who having been ordained two years earlier to the priesthood had dropped, as was the custom, his secular name "Constantine" and adopted "Cyril" as his ecclesiastical name. This was a name which had been rendered illustrious by a great predecessor of his in the See of Alexandria. So from now on he will be known to us as Cyril Lucaris.

We know very little about his ordination; even the exact year in which that event took place is uncertain.[1] Of one thing we are fairly sure, that Cyril was ordained in Constantinople. There are many conjectures about the course Cyril followed after leaving Padua. Some writers are of the opinion that he visited various countries of Europe before returning to his homeland.[2] But this seems rather doubtful. These writers seem to have confused the Latin name of Padua, *Patavium,* with that of Holland, *Batavia,* and have sent Cyril on a most doubtful journey to that distant land. However this may be, Cyril eventually found himself in Constantinople, where his uncle Meletios Pegas, Patriarch of Alexandria, was then locum tenens of the vacant Ecumenical Throne.[3] And it was at the hands of his old uncle and benefactor, who had cherished so many hopes for him in his student days in Padua, that Cyril received the priesthood.[4] The fact that we now find him in Brest, and entrusted at this early stage of his career with a delicate and difficult mission, is evidence that old Meletios still had great ambitions for his nephew and esteemed his ability highly. In order to understand better the character of this mission, we must first cast a glance at the state of ecclesiastical affairs in Poland at that time.

Sigismund III, son of John III of Sweden, was reigning in the year 1596. He had been born to John III and Catherine Jagello while the former was kept in prison by his brother Eric. Sigismund had now been reigning for nine years and had had plenty of time to express his great aversion for any other form of the Christian faith than the one which his Catholic mother had taught him. And this royal dislike was not slow in making itself felt in the public life of the country. Sigismund was by no means the first to put his royal authority at the disposal of the Catholic Church for the promotion of the Counter Reformation movement in Poland. It was his predecessor, Stephen Bathory, who had dealt the first heavy blows against Protestantism in Poland and had prepared the way for the Roman Church to assume once again supremacy in that country. Like Henry of Navarre, Stephen had given up his Protestant faith in order to become King, and although opinions about him differ,[5] he seems to have been inclined by temperament toward a policy of moderation in church affairs. But even if he was so disposed, he was prevented by the queen, the bishops, and the special envoy of the Holy See from acting according to his intention. And so, probably against his better judgment, he was gradually driven to a policy of undisguised protection of the Roman faith at the expense of the Protestant and the Greek Orthodox Churches.[6]

It was before Stephen's accession to the throne that the Jesuits had entered Poland, through the aid of Cardinal Hosius, Bishop of Ermeland, who in 1569 had founded a college for them in Brannsberg.[7] But it was chiefly under Stephen Bathory that this Society realized its first big successes in Poland. Thanks to the liberality of the royal treasury the Jesuits were able to fill the land with their colleges—placed at Riga and Dorpat, at Wilna and Polock, at Pultusk and Lublin—so that before long the Society of Jesus numbered as many as three hundred and sixty members in the country. Not without reason did the Jesuits call the ex-Protestant King *"Pater et patronus noster."*[8]

Things were brought to a climax, however, under his successor, Sigismund III. What Stephen started as a matter of policy, Sigismund continued out of deep personal conviction, and in his reign new measures were taken for the promotion of the Roman Catholic conquest of the country. When Clement VIII was still a cardinal and a legate in Poland, he had advised Sigismund, then a prince, not to entrust public offices to any save to Roman Catholics. This advice was not forgotten by Sigismund when he came to the throne; and the better to estimate the effectiveness of the weapon now in the hands of the reactionary forces in the country one has to note that not less than twenty thousand offices, spiritual and temporal, were "in the gift of the king." This new measure was not slow in bringing about the desired results, and so men, especially of the upper classes, Protestant as well as Greek Orthodox, driven by the force of circumstances, gradually found their way into the Roman fold. Clement VIII was right when he ascribed the progress of Roman Catholicism in Poland chiefly to the measure which he himself had advocated.[9]

While this measure was bearing its fruit, another blow fell with great force on the Greek Orthodox element. This was the decision to exclude all non-Roman bishops from a seat in the senate. The situation thus created was received by the Greek Orthodox clergy with great bitterness while it proved of great benefit to the Roman Catholic Church.[10] The life of the Greek Orthodox Church was being made more and more difficult and, strange as it may seem, matters got worse as a result of a visit paid to Poland by the highest authority of this church itself. It would take us too far afield to enter into the details of that visit. Suffice it to say that a rivalry existed between the Greek Orthodox clergy and the Confraternities in Poland at a time when the danger of a Roman invasion made it imperative that all elements within the Church should unite in a common effort. To make matters worse, an ugly scandal of immorality in connection with the Bishop of Loutsk suddenly broke out. But, above all, there was the permanent evil of the very low educational standard, even illiteracy in many cases, of the Greek Orthodox clergy, who could not compete with the vastly better educated clergy of the Roman Church. It was in order to deal with the situation which arose out of the combination of these evil factors in the Church that Jeremiah, Patriarch of Constantinople, paid a visit to Poland and Russia. Jeremiah was a good man, one of the few bright exceptions in the long list of unworthy men who at that time occupied the Ecumenical Throne. During his visit to Poland, however, he did not show much administrative ability—but then the Greek Orthodox clergy were never very good statesmen, in sharp contrast to their brethren within the Roman Church. And when his visit came to an end, Jeremiah left matters in a worse state than before. Shortly afterward he died, and his successors seem to have done very little to improve this bad situation. Thus when the Roman danger appeared, the Greek Orthodox Church in Poland had to face it practically unaided—practically but not quite, as the presence of Cyril Lucaris and Nicephorus Cantacuzinos in Poland at that time testifies.

Of Cyril's movements in Poland we cannot speak with certainty, as our sources are not in accord about them.[11] It is certain, however, that in the execution of his difficult mission he undertook several journeys to Poland, that he spent nearly five years there, and that it was in Poland that he had the first of his numerous encounters with the Roman Church—encounters which were to continue during the whole of his adventurous career. He came to Poland as an "exarch," a special envoy of the Patriarch of Alexandria, while Cantacuzinos acted as an exarch of the Patriarch of Constantinople. Meletios Pegas considered this mission so important that he would have gone to Poland in person had not urgent business kept him in Constantinople. So Lucaris had been dispatched in his stead. Cyril arrived in Poland just when the situation had reached its sinister climax, just after the Roman bomb had exploded in Brest—too late to avert it, but not late enough to be safe from the explosion. He came too late to take part in the first Council of Brest which took place in 1595, and just in time to participate in the second which was held the following year. But the fate of the Church had already been sealed.

We have already seen how bitterly the higher Greek Orthodox clergy felt about their exclusion from the senate because of their religious convictions. And as things grew worse, with the passing of time an influential party grew within the Church, under the leadership of Michael the Metropolitan of the Greek Orthodox Church in Poland and Ignatius Potsi the Bishop of Vladimir, which advocated union with Rome according to the terms of the Synod of Florence. Secret negotiations were held which lasted for five years, the result of which was the first Council of Brest held in June 1595. During this Council it was agreed that the Polish Church should submit to the authority of the Pope and accept the doctrine of the Roman Church, retaining, however, the Eastern form of liturgy, Communion in both forms, the Julian calendar, and the marriage of the priesthood. In consequence, bishops were commissioned by the Council to proceed to Rome and submit to the Pope the allegiance of the Polish Church. Pope Clement VIII, who had already been looking at this Polish affair as a steppingstone to an Eastward drive as far as China and India, needed no persuasion to extend his Apostolic pardon to these erring children. And thus it was that two days before Christmas 1595 and in the midst of great jubilation the Uniate was born in Rome.[12]

When the report reached Poland, horror struck in the hearts of the masses who had remained faithful to the Greek Orthodox tradition. A wave of anger swept the country against those spiritual leaders who had betrayed their trust. And when a second Council convened at Brest in order to ratify the agreement of Rome, it was attended by great numbers of those who had remained loyal to the Greek Orthodox Church. It was at this Council that the exarchs of the Eastern Patriarchates presented themselves. The Greek Orthodox party within the Council was headed by the famous Voivoda of Kieff, the hundred-year-old Prince Constantine of Ostrogg. To this man the Greek Orthodox Church in Russia, at the time of Ivan the Terrible, owed the first printed edition of the Bible and other sacred books in the Slavonic language. The fate of the Council, however, had been decided beforehand. The Romanist party, though hardly as numerous as its opponents, had the protection of the King, which put them at an advantage. The Council soon split into two smaller assemblies, the one attended by the Unionists, who met in the Church of the Virgin where Te Deums were sung in thanksgiving for the happy conclusion of this matter, and the other by the anti-Unionists,

who held their meetings in a private house, where a solemn protest against the treachery of the Unionist bishops was passed.
Then the two rival assemblies promptly proceeded to anathematize each other.[13]

It is evident from the above that Cyril's share in facing the
crisis which had suddenly broken out within the Church in
Poland was very small. Apart from the encouragement which the
presence of the special envoy of the See of Alexandria gave to
those who had remained loyal to the Greek Orthodox Church,
his arrival had little more to offer at that late hour of the day.
But even those who had sent the two exarchs could hardly expect
them to be of any real help to the troubled Church at that late
date. The most they could hope for was that their delegates would
be able to save some of the wreckage from the great storm which
had broken out within the Church. This Cyril endeavored to do;
and in dealing with the situation with which he was confronted
he gives us the first evidence of the farsightedness of a man who
prefers methods which require time to yield sure results to
methods which promise spectacular but short-lived success.

It did not take Cyril long to realize that the one great defect
of the Greek Orthodox Church, which placed it in a position of
disadvantage as against the Roman Church, was the very low
educational standard both of its laymen and of the majority of
its clergy. In a letter written about this time, a fellow worker of
his, Gabriel Dorotheides, says, "The Greek Orthodox population
of Poland is scoffed at by outsiders for their ignorance," and
"Many there are who as a result of this ignorance are driven to
other forms of faith."[14] In the case of many priests, ignorance was
accompanied by poverty, which naturally placed the Greek Orthodox clergy at a disadvantage in relation to the well-provided-for
clergy of the Roman Church. In another letter this same priest,
Dorotheides, complains that he could not go to visit Cyril because
it was raining very hard and, having no shoes, he could not wade
through the mud.[15]

Cyril saw that if he wanted to do something of lasting value
for the Church in Poland, he had to start at the beginning—and
this he did. He devoted the five years which he spent in that

country to the improvement of schools of the Greek Orthodox community and to the setting up of a printing house in order to publish the books which the people so urgently needed.

He started work at Wilna, much to the regret of Dorotheides, who lived at Lwow and had strongly urged Cyril to come and work there, indicating in glowing terms that the opportunities which Lwow offered for such work were far greater than in Wilna.[16] Cyril worked for twenty months as the Rector of the Greek Orthodox School in Wilna,[17] and it was there that he set up his printing house. We are not surprised to find that among the first books he published was one by his own uncle Meletios Pegas, "whose authority," as Cyril himself wrote in the foreword, "not Egypt alone, but the whole of Greece is ready to obey."[18]

While in Wilna, Cyril did not forget the needs of the believers in other parts of the country, especially those of his friend Dorotheides, to whom he offered through his frequent letters a course of studies which included readings from Aristotle.[19] One can therefore imagine the joy of the latter, when at the end of twenty months Cyril left Wilna and came to work in Lwow. But whereas Cyril had been the Rector of the already existing school at Wilna, he had to found a Greek school in Lwow; this we gather from a letter of Pegas to the Bishop of Lwow.[20] In this way Cyril worked for the education of the Greek Orthodox people in Poland.

This work was carried on under circumstances of great hardship and in an environment of unconcealed hostility. At one time a letter from a friend warns him not to come to Lwow at that particular time for reasons which the writer said he did not dare to specify.[21] On another occasion his mail from Egypt is withheld by friends lest it should fall into the hands of enemies.[22] On still another occasion he complains that he cannot proceed to Ostrow.[23] At one time the rumor was spread in Lwow by the Romanist party that Meletios Pegas himself had submitted to Rome, and as was to be expected, this created great confusion among the Greek Orthodox flock in that city.[24] And the terror and confusion were intensified when the news came that Nicephorus, the Exarch of the Patriarch of Constantinople, had been arrested and put to death by order of Sigismund.[25] At this time Cyril himself was in danger of being arrested and so had to flee for his life and seek the protection of Prince Constantine Basil, in whose castle he spent some time.[26] In the midst of so much work and diverse dangers he did not neglect his own reading, and among the authors he read at that time were Thomas Aquinas and the historian Cedrinos.[27]

Cyril's stay in Poland was not uninterrupted. During those unsettled times he must have felt the need for consultations with his superiors, and so we find him on August 6, 1598, preaching in Callipolis of Thrace, and on Christmas eve of the same year in Crete.[28] When he returned to Poland in 1599 he was the bearer of a letter to King Sigismund himself. Sigismund had written to Pegas asking him to submit to the authority of the Pope and to accept the doctrine of the Roman Church for the sake of peace within the Church of Christ. It was the Patriarch's answer to this request that Cyril brought to the King—a mission not free from danger, considering the contents of the letter and the temperament of its recipient. The Patriarch, however, committed the safety of "the Reverend Father Cyril, Exarch of this Apostolic See and a son of ours" to the clemency of the King.[29]

Cyril did not prolong his stay in Poland. He realized that under the existing conditions he could not offer much more to the cause of his church in that country. On the other hand, the call of his homeland came to him once more through his uncle Meletios. In an earlier letter the uncle had given to his nephew a prophetic hint about the future: "The Throne (of Alexandria) does not ask anything of thine, but thyself."[30] And now that he feels the end approaching, Meletios gives his nephew his last injunctions. "My son Cyril," he writes, "I have come to the end of my life. I have tasted pains and dangers and worries and I am dying a happy man . . . One counsel I have to give thee: Fight to preserve the faith. . . . I have known thee to be faithful, but, loving thee as I do, I could not restrain myself from giving superfluous counsel."[31] That was enough for Cyril; as soon as possible he started on his journey to Egypt.

His enemies in Poland, however, did not let him go without dealing him a last blow. A letter was forged by Peter Scarga, the leader of the Jesuits in that country, purporting to be written by

Cyril and addressed to the Roman Catholic Bishop of Lwow, Demetrius Solicowski, in which, after referring to "the See of St. Peter" with much reverence, Cyril expresses the hope that the union of the Eastern with the Western Church will some time be effected.[32] The forgery of this letter is evident. Lucaris himself vehemently denied having written it.[33] Then, the contents of this letter are in sharp contradiction both to the struggles which Cyril had conducted for five whole years in Poland and to his character as it is known to us. Even if we were to suppose that Cyril had been obliged to write such a letter in order to purchase security for himself, we would expect this letter to make its appearance at the time when he had been traveling all over Poland in the midst of great dangers, when his fellow worker Nicephorus had been put to death, rather than at the time of his departure to the safety of Egypt. And, finally, if the letter were genuine, why did not Scarga or Solicowski bring it to light immediately, and thus deal a heavy blow to the Greek Orthodox Church in Poland, instead of waiting, as they did, seventeen whole years before they published it?

So Cyril left the land of his first labors. On his way back he visited the Greek Orthodox communities in Rumania,[34] where he preached the Word, and on the 11th of September 1601 he was in Egypt.[35]

Two days later Meletios Pegas died.[36]

CHAPTER 5

PATRIARCH OF ALEXANDRIA

N O SOONER HAD CYRIL SET FOOT on Egyptian soil than he experienced one of the greatest moments in his life. The orphaned church immediately elected him to be the successor of Meletios Pegas, and thus in 1601 Cyril was raised to the See of Alexandria at the age of twenty-nine.[1] This was a wise election, and Cyril held this responsible office for twenty years, until he was called to an even more responsible one.

Cyril's elevation to the Throne of Alexandria is a convenient point at which to introduce into our narrative one who spared no pains in maligning his memory.* In connection with Cyril's election to the Throne of Alexandria, Leo Allatius in his *De Ecclesiae Occidentalis et Orientalis Perpetua Consensione* accuses Cyril of having bought the throne with money he had collected for the needs of the Church of Alexandria, while the majority of the bishops were in favor of the election of Gerasimos Spartaliotes. That this is a calumny with no historical foundation whatever is proved by the fact that after his election and all through his life Cyril enjoyed the friendship and the esteem of Spartaliotes, with whom he kept up friendly correspondence

* Leo Allatius, a Greek Roman Catholic and contemporary of Lucaris, born in the island of Chios, was brought to Rome while yet a child and became one of the most distinguished pupils of the Greek College of St. Athanasius. Pope Alexander VII appointed him keeper of the Vatican library, and here he spent the rest of his life writing books. He was a man of great learning, and it is a pity that in his zeal for the promotion of the cause so near to his heart, the submission of the Greek Church to the Pope, he on several occasions deliberately introduced falsehoods in his writings. He has earned, not without justice, the title "Doctor Falsiloquus,"[2] and John Covel[3] preserved a saying of Dositheus according to which Allatius at his deathbed ate his own tongue, in his agony for the many lies which that tongue had told.

when he was elevated to the Throne of Constantinople and the
latter occupied the Throne of Alexandria. This would never have
happened had Spartaliotes known that Cyril had deprived him of
his election to the See of Alexandria by such means as those
attributed to him by Allatius.

It was a difficult task which Cyril had now before him. The
Church in Egypt was anything but flourishing at the time of his
elevation to the See. It is true that his love for the Church of
which he was the pastor caused him to speak of it with great
pride, and to compare it with the Church of Constantinople,
much to the disadvantage of the latter, stressing the fact that
the Church of Alexandria had managed to preserve its independence from the Turks.[4] All these boasts, however, related mostly
to the past, for at the time of Cyril's arrival the Church in
Alexandria had already been on the decline for a long time.
The Greek Orthodox population of Egypt had been steadily
diminishing; their communities were small islands in an ever-
increasing sea of Copts, and the three or four Metropolitans
who surrounded the Patriarch had nominal rather than actual
authority.[5] Cyril himself in his letter of October 10, 1613, to
Uytenbogaert,[6] speaking of the Copts in Egypt, says that one
could use the words of Homer who writes of the Greeks and
Trojans: "καὶ πολλαίκεν δεκάδες δείατο οἰνοχόϊο"; that is, the number
of the Copts would be ten times as large as that of the Greek
Orthodox. An amusing detail in this letter of Cyril's is his unexpected etymology of the word "Copt." "They call them Copts,"
he says, "because they circumcise themselves." One would expect
Cyril to know the real derivation of this word—from the word
"Egypt."

The Copts were not Cyril's only problem while in Alexandria.
In his letter to David Le Leu de Wilhem of March 20, 1618, he
complains that the Nestorians, who fifty years before were almost
nonexistent in the country, had now spread over the whole of the
land and had come into close fellowship with the Copts, "the
blind with those who are equally blind."[7] In his letter to Uytenbogaert mentioned above, he characterizes this sect as the one
most infected by heresy and calls its followers the "pests of the
Orient." If this language is too strong for the head of a church

to use, it can only be explained as an indication of Cyril's disappointment over the decline of the once flourishing Greek Orthodox Church in Egypt, in contrast to the "heresies" whose followers were steadily increasing.

Soon after his arrival in Egypt, Cyril took up his official residence in Cairo. This must have been another sad reminder to him of the decline of the Church of Alexandria. In his letter to Uytenbogaert he attributes the change of residence to the better climate of Cairo, but De la Croix ascribes this to the larger degree of freedom which the Christians had in that city.[8] And George Sandys gives the real explanation when he says that the "Metropolis of Africa . . . now hath nothing left her but ruines. . . . the buildings now being, are meane and few, errected on the ruines of the former: that part that lyeth along the shore inhabited onely, the rest desolate."[9] That is how it came to pass that the once famous city of Alexandria could no longer serve as the official residence of the successors of the great Athanasius and Cyril.

If, however, residence in Cairo lacked the historical atmosphere of Alexandria, the lack was made up by the luxuries of one of the great modern cities of that time. Sandys in his *Relation of a Journey* tells how greatly impressed he was by the beauties of the city. "Than Cairo no City can be more populous, nor better served with all sorts of provision. Here hatche they egges by artificial heate in infinite numbers"—and he goes on to give a minute description of this wonderful thing.[10] The beautiful houses, the "magnificent Mosques," the "Santons," or lodgings for "fooles and mad men," of whom, it appears, Cairo had more than its fair share, the "Serraglios" of the important people, the women "too fine-fingered to meddle with housewifry, riding abroad upon pleasure on eassie-going Asses," the great variety of public amusements, such as "the Raven which spoke" and the goat that performed acrobatic feats, the camel that danced and the ass that did such tricks "as if possessed with reasons," made Cairo one of the great cities of the world.

We may doubt, however, whether Cyril, while in that great city, had much time to spare for the raven that spoke or the ass that did tricks. He was much too busy for that. It is a pity that we have so little information about his life in Egypt; such infor-

mation as we do have, however, gives us a picture of an ever-
growing and ever-expanding activity.

The information we have about his first years in Egypt is especially poor. We know, however, that as soon as he was established
in the See he started preaching. He realized that one of the greatest enemies which he had to fight against was the ignorance of
his own people. For this reason he was a preacher throughout
his career. Many of the sermons which he preached at that time
have come down to us. We have, for example, fifty-two of the
sermons he preached in Cairo in the years 1609 and 1610. And
there are others which he preached at different times during that
early period of his work.[11] The years 1608 and 1609 were taken
up by another kind of activity. When Cyril was elected Patriarch
he found the See heavily burdened with debts. On the other hand
the need for some buildings was urgent if the Church was to
accomplish its work. Cyril, therefore, sent the monk Maximus
Peloponnesius on a tour to the Churches of Greece and Russia
to collect funds for the Church of Alexandria. As soon as the first
proceeds of Maximus' labors were received in Cairo, Cyril immediately started on his building program. This effort, however,
came to an abrupt end, for Maximus was seized by pirates and
his tour was cut short.[12]

At an earlier date Cyril had occasion to visit the island of
Cyprus. The Church in that island was passing through some
trouble at that time. In 1600 Athanasius, the Archbishop of
Cyprus, was deposed by the Ecumenical Patriarch, and Benjamin,
a capable and good priest, was elected in his place. The deposed
Archbishop and his party persecuted Benjamin, however, and
finally succeeded in driving him from the island. Thus the Church
in Cyprus found itself without a leader, and the notables of the
island asked Cyril to come and help them. In answer to this appeal Cyril went to Cyprus, and we have a few sermons preached
by him there during that troubled period.[13] After long deliberation, Cyril ordained Christodulus as the Archbishop of the
island,[14] an office which Christodulus held for thirty-two years.

Shortly afterward Cyril was called to Jerusalem in order to
take part in the induction of the Patriarch of Jerusalem, Theophanes (1608-1644), with whom he established a close and last-

ing friendship. While in Jerusalem, Cyril had the opportunity of visiting the Holy Sepulchre. He expressed himself quite strongly against the ornaments with which people, in their religious zeal, had through the years disfigured the cave in which the dead body of our Lord had lain.[15] Could this be an indication that Cyril's thought had begun to move along paths of a more simple Christian faith?

In 1602, one year after his elevation to the Throne of Alexandria, he renewed an earlier acquaintance which was destined to prove of great importance in his life. At the time when Cyril was still a priest he had met a Dutchman, Cornelius van Haga, who was then traveling in the Levant. Van Haga had now been appointed envoy of the "States General" to the Porte Sublime, and he came to Constantinople, where he met his old acquaintance, now Patriarch of Alexandria. Cyril entreated Van Haga to provide him with some books written by Protestant divines, a request which was promptly passed on to Holland. And shortly afterward Cyril received his first set of books of Protestant theology.[16]

We cannot know with certainty what the immediate results of the study of those books were. A few years later, however, Cyril came into contact, again through the intermediacy of Cornelius van Haga, with the famous Dutch theologian J. Uytenbogaert, who had just succeeded Jacob Arminius in the leadership of the famous Remonstrant school of theology. It is very interesting to note in Cyril's correspondence of this period his gradual but steady progress toward an Evangelical belief.

As early as October 1613, in his letter to J. Uytenbogaert,[17] he speaks of the sacraments as being only two in number. And he does not attribute to them, as such, any effectual power, but states that they can confer grace only if accompanied by faith. He hastens, however, to add that faith has no power to save without the aid of the sacraments. Speaking more specifically of the sacrament of Baptism, he says that it cannot save if it is not accompanied by repentance; his exact meaning, however, is not very clear. There is also some confusion in his mind concerning the sacrament of the Lord's Supper. He says: "This Sacrament has been given us in order that we may celebrate the memory of the

Lord's death and receive His body and blood." That he still accepted the doctrine of a change in essence is evident, for further down in the same letter he quotes a prayer offered at the Lord's Supper with the supplication that the bread and wine should be changed into the body and blood of Christ. And there is no word of censure against the use of this prayer.

In the same letter, however, he makes a great concession to the Protestant faith when he admits the existence of certain erroneous practices within the Greek Church, "which," he says, "we cannot remove on account of great difficulties." "But," he adds, "in contrast to the Roman, the Greek Church does not regard these practices, which have not been expressly ordained by God, as necessary unto salvation; on the contrary she holds that they are liable to error. Inasmuch as only that which God Himself has ordained is infallible, all such practices must be submitted to the scrutiny of the Scriptures and of the Holy Spirit."

Another famous Protestant divine, with whom Cyril came in contact, was David Le Leu de Wilhem, a Dutchman who later became a member of the Council of the Princes of Orange and Brabant. While traveling in the Levant during the years 1617, 1618, and 1619 he had in Cairo the opportunity of visiting Lucaris, with whom he later kept up a correspondence. In a letter to De Wilhem, Cyril stresses the unique position in which he holds the Scriptures as the rule of the Christian faith.[18] His silence concerning tradition is very eloquent, as one would expect a Greek Orthodox theologian to place tradition alongside the Scriptures as a factor in the rule of faith. It seems that by this time, Cyril's theological outlook had begun to be distinctly different from that of a Greek Orthodox divine. In his next letter to De Wilhem,[19] he gives thanks to God for "he can state with confidence that in the essentials of the faith he is in agreement with him" ("$Εἰς$ $τὰ$ $καίρια$ $τῆς$ $πίστεως$ $συμφωνοῦμεν$")—a remarkable statement, in view of the great dogmatic divergencies existing between the Greek Orthodox position and that of the Protestant Church. In the same letter he enumerates the things which should take place if the Greek Church is to be reformed, and among these he lists "the Evangelical simplicity" which should take the place of "supersition," for, he adds, nothing brings more disgrace on the Greek Church than its superstitions. This same subject of the reform of the Greek Church is touched upon in a later letter in which Cyril expresses, in very strong language, both his desire for such a reform and his doubts concerning its feasibility.[20]

There is some obscurity concerning Cyril's position in connection with the Lord's Supper. In another letter to De Wilhem,[21] he says that as regards this point he can distinguish three schools of doctrine: (a) the Papist, (b) the Lutheran, and (c) the Orthodox, and that so far as he is concerned, he follows the Orthodox. One wonders whether he makes here any distinction between the Lutheran and the Calvinist schools, and whether he identifies the Orthodox position with the Calvinist one. The text of his letter does not allow any definite conclusions to be drawn; the above assumption, however, is rendered more likely by the fact that at that time—and even to this present day, so far as terminology at least is concerned—the Greek Orthodox Church did not take the same rigid attitude regarding the form of change as the Roman Church. In support of the above supposition comes another letter from Cyril to the same person, on March 13, 1619,[22] in which he expresses his joy that as regards the Lord's Supper he is of one mind with De Wilhem. Some element of ambiguity, however, is introduced when he says that he who participates in the Lord's Supper, animated by faith, "partakes not only of the visible Sacrament of the Body and Blood, but also in a *spiritual* way, of the body and blood of Jesus Christ."

The extent of the change between Cyril's present way of thinking and that of earlier days, can be noticed most clearly in his letter to Mark Antonio de Dominis, who though formerly a Roman Catholic Archbishop had later embraced the Protestant faith. In this letter bearing the date of September 6, 1618, he says: "There was a time, when we were bewitched, before we understood the very pure Word of God; and although we did not communicate with the Roman Pontiff . . . we abominated the doctrine of the Reformed Churches, as opposed to the Faith, not knowing in good truth what we abominated. But when it pleased the merciful God to enlighten us, and make us perceive our former error, we began to consider what our future stand should be. And as the role of a good citizen, in the case of any dissension, is to defend the juster cause, I think it all the more to be the duty of a good Christian not to dissimulate his sentiments in matters pertaining to salvation, but to embrace unreservedly that side which is most accordant to the Word of God. What did I do then? Having obtained, through the kindness of friends, some writings of Evangelical theologians, books which have not only been unseen in the East, but, due to the influence of the censures of Rome, have not even been heard of, I then invoked earnestly the assistance of the Holy Ghost, and for three years compared the doctrines of the Greek and Latin Churches with that of the Reformed. . . . Leaving the Fathers I took for my only guide the Scriptures and the Analogy of Faith. At length, having been convinced, through the grace of God, that the cause of the Reformers was more correct and more in accord with the doctrine of Christ, I embraced it. I can no longer bear to hear men say that the comments of human tradition are of equal weight with Holy Scripture. . . . In the Sacrament of the Lord's Supper we fully believe that Christ is present, not illusorily and symbolically, but truly and in person, substantially and really, as is testified by the Word of our Lord, 'which is given for you.' With respect to the manner of the Presence, our Greek Church is at variance both with those who adopt the chimera of transubstantiation, and with the erroneous opinion of the Ubiquitaries. . . . As for Image Worship, it is impossible for me to say how disastrous it is under the present circumstances. . . . not that I can say that, absolutely speaking, images are to be condemned, since, when not worshipped, they cannot do any harm; but I abhor the idolatry of which they are the cause to these blind worshippers. And although in my private prayers I have sometimes observed that the Crucifix was an assistance to my mind, as bringing more readily before it the Passion of our Lord, yet in view of the fact that the naive, to say nothing of some who are enlightened, are carried away from the true and spiritual worship and adoration which is due to God alone, I would rather that all would entirely abstain from this so dangerous handle of sin. . . . As for the invocation of Saints, there was a time when I too did not perceive how it overshadowed the glory of our Lord Christ. . . ."[23]

Speaking of Cyril's theological position, it is interesting to note the various theological questions which occupied his mind at that time. In his letter to Uytenbogaert, of October 10, 1613,[24] he asks the latter to supply him with a list of commentators on various books of the Bible, with a Confession of his faith and an interpretation of the ceremonies which are observed in the Reformed churches, as well as a statement of their administration and discipline. At this time he seems to be mainly occupied with the big questions of "free will" and "predestination."[25] In a letter to De Wilhem, dated May 10, 1619,[26] he confesses that he finds this a most difficult problem and asks whether De Wilhem could send him a book on this subject. Later on he comes back to this subject and promises to write something on it himself.[27]

Another question with which he dealt in his correspondence with his friends at this time was the famous *Filioque*, and in the handling of this subject he showed himself a deep thinker and an able debater.[28] He rejects the addition to the article of the Creed dealing with the Holy Spirit which the churches in the West had made and affirms in a very able way that when we speak of the procession of the Holy Spirit from the Father we mean that the Father is the Source in which the third Person of the Godhead has its "hypostatic essence" and that if we were to accept that the Holy Spirit proceeded from the Son as well, it would be as if we accepted that the Holy Spirit has His "source of essence" in two different principles. He is unwilling to accept this "absurdity," as he calls it; he accepts, however, that the Holy Spirit, who has His source of being in the Father, is being given to mankind through the Son.

To the second half of Cyril's term in Alexandria belong the journeys which brought him to Contantinople, Mount Athos, and Moldovlahia. Early in 1611 we find him in Constantinople; this we gather from sermons which he preached in that city in January and February of that year.[29] Later in the year he is back in Cairo for a stay of a few months only, and early in 1612 he is once again in Constantinople. The Ecumenical Patriarch Neophytus II had been deposed because of the support which he had given to the activities of the Jesuits in Constantinople, and Cyril was called to act as locum tenens just as his uncle, Meletios Pegas, had done on a previous occasion.[30] In a short time the election took place. Cyril, being one of the candidates, would certainly have been appointed Ecumenical Patriarch had he consented to pay the large sum of money which the Turkish government required in order to ratify his election.[31] But as Cyril did not consent to do this, his opponent, Timothy II, occupied the Throne. The party spirit ran very high in Constantinople on that occasion, and Cyril found that his life would be in danger at the hands of Timothy and his followers if he were to return to Egypt, so he betook himself to Mount Athos, where he spent some time with the monks there.[32] When he realized that even there he was not safe from the plots of Timothy II, he was obliged to take refuge in Tergoviste, of Vlachia, where he was received cordially and given hospitality by Prince Voivoda Radu Michnea, who had been a fellow student of his in Venice. The real cause of Timothy's enmity was his jealousy of an opponent far more able than himself; he disguised this, however, under the excuse that Cyril had become a follower of Luther and was therefore dangerous to the Church. While still in Vlachia, Cyril replied to these accusations of Timothy's.[33] His arguments, however, were of such a nature as to do nothing but confirm Timothy's accusation. "And as for the accusation that I am a Lutheran," he says, "it is not to be wondered at that he who neither knows, nor has dreamt of Luther's religion and wisdom, and is ignorant of the points of agreement and disagreement between the Greek Orthodox Church and the Lutherans, should fall into a pit."

A very interesting page of the history of the Greek Church of that time is connected with Cyril's stay in Mount Athos. In the monastery where he stayed he met a seventeen-year-old boy from Berroea of Macedonia named Metrophanes Critopoulos. Cyril was deeply impressed by this boy's love for learning, and on his return to Egypt he took the boy along with him and there ordained him a priest. At that time Cyril received through Archbishop Abbot of Canterbury an offer from King James I of England to have a few Greek young men study theology in England.[34] Cyril could not desire a better candidate for this than the boy from Mount Athos. This young man, who was destined to succeed Cyril on the throne of Alexandria and to adorn the Church with his culture, was speedily dispatched to England. Early in 1618 Cyril received a letter from Archbishop Abbot, in which this

prelate wrote: ". . . Your young Metrophanes' name has been inscribed on the roll of the students of the University of Oxford,
and when the young plant grows and brings forth good fruit, it
will be reserved to your wisdom to decide whether he will remain
in this country or will be transplanted to his native land."[35]

It would take us too far afield to follow this remarkable young
man's career. Suffice it to say that he justified all the best hopes
that Cyril had for him. When Critopoulos finished his studies in
Oxford, Cyril entrusted him with the task of visiting certain parts
of western Europe in order to get better acquainted with the Reformed faith as it was practiced in those countries. Critopoulos
accordingly informed Archbishop Abbot that he would return to
Constantinople by the overland route through the Continent and
not by ship. Because of this decision the Archbishop was infuriated with his former protégé and declared that he would have
nothing to do with him in the future. Furthermore, he wrote to
the English ambassador in Constantinople, Sir Thomas Roe, giving vent to his indignation against Critopoulos and against the
whole Greek nation, whose ingratitude he deplored in very strong
terms. It is hard to tell whether the wrath of the Archbishop
against Critopoulos was roused by his fear of the cost of the
journey by the overland route, as he himself maintained, or by
his jealousy of Critopoulos, who, without the assistance of the
former had gained entrance into the Royal Palace and enjoyed
the favor of the King.[36] Critopoulos, however, proceeded to carry
out Cyril's orders and started on his journey back to Egypt
through the Continent. He visited the most important centers of
Protestant teaching in Germany and Switzerland, gave lectures
in their universities, published at the request of one of their
divines a Confession of his faith, and arrived at last in Venice,
where he remained for some time, having instructions to publish
there some of the works of Cyril. In this, however, he was not
successful, for he met with the opposition of the Venetian authorities, and so he sailed for Constantinople, having been away from
his homeland for thirteen years. He disappears from our narrative
for the time being but he will make another appearance on a
very sad occasion.

CHAPTER 6

ON THE ECUMENICAL THRONE

". . . Having been assembled in the Church of the Patriarchate, dedicated to St. George, we proceeded to the election for the vacant holy and high throne of Constantinople . . . and we elected . . . his holiness Cyril, a man famous for his virtue and wisdom."[1] In such terms the Holy Synod in Constantinople, under the chairmanship of the Metropolitan of Heracleia, in conformity to tradition, announced to the Christian world the election of Cyril Lucaris to the Ecumenical Throne. The date of this document, according to Legrand, is November 4, 1620. Other contemporary authorities, however, give the date as November 5, 1621. The latter appears to be the most probable date.[2]

Cyril's election to the See of Constantinople was too good an opportunity for Allatius' lying tongue to miss. He therefore invented the story that the death of Cyril's predecessor Timothy was caused by poison, which Cyril's friend, the Dutch ambassador in Constantinople, gave him at a banquet to which he had been invited, thus vacating the throne for Cyril to occupy. Slanders of this sort against the memory of Cyril and his friends are to be found quite often in the writings of Allatius.[3]

While still Patriarch of Alexandria, Cyril had expressed himself with great disapproval, as we saw,[4] concerning the intervention of the Turkish authorities in the election and induction of the Patriarch of Constantinople. And now Cyril was to have a personal experience of this humiliating state of things, as his first public action after his election was the payment to the Turkish authorities of the *peshkesh*, a sum of money, without the payment of which he could not enter upon the duties of his office. This in itself was very humiliating, and it was rendered even more so for

Cyril by the knowledge that it had been brought about by the pettiness and the narrow-mindedness of his own fellow country-men.

The relations of the Greek Church with the Turkish authorities had not always been of such a humiliating nature for the Church. When Mohammed II conquered Constantinople, in 1453, he declared his policy of full freedom of conscience for the Greeks and expressed the desire to meet the head of the Greek Church. The Patriarch, however, was dead, and as no other official of the Church was available, George Scholarius, a man famous for his erudition, was brought before the Sultan, and gave him all the information he required about the Greek Church and its practices. The Sultan was so pleased with the replies which Scholarius gave him that he caused him to be elevated to the vacant office of Patriarch under the name of Gennadius.[5] The Sultan himself placed the Pastoral Staff in Gennadius' hand, and gave him the black vest of his office and a white horse. The newly appointed Patriarch, seated on his white horse and accompanied by a great number of Turkish officials and representatives of the Greek Church, was led to the Patriarchal seat.[6] This happy state of things was not of long duration. Only four Patriarchs—Gennadius, Isidorus, Joasaph, and Mark Xilokaravis enjoyed the privileges granted by Mohammed II. After the fall of Trebizond two rival parties, equally strong, were formed in Constantinople: the old Constantinopolitan and the Trapezuntine. When the Trapezuntines felt that they had sufficient power in their hands, they strove to place a member of their own party on the Patriarchal Throne, and since they could not accomplish this through a majority of votes in the Synod, they did it by means of bribery. They sent the sum of one thousand florins to the Sultan with the request that he should appoint Symeon, one of their number, to be the Patriarch. When the Sultan heard the request, he laughed, wondering at the stupidity of the Greeks, and immediately ordered that Symeon should be inducted as Patriarch.[7]

This was the beginning, and things went rapidly from bad to worse. On the one hand this new method opened the way for the ambition of any party or person within the Greek Church to override the lawful procedure of appointing the head of the Church.

On the other hand it opened new ways of exploitation on the part of Turkish officials at a time when venality had very deeply corrupted the Turkish state. The Turkish officials were only too quick to grasp this opportunity. Khotsibeg, who lived at about the time when Cyril arrived in Constantinople, wrote a treatise on the causes which brought about the decline of the Ottoman Empire, and attributed this decline to the increase of venality.[8] Before 1598 nobody could be appointed as a civil servant unless he belonged as a *danishmend* or pupil to a *medresse*—a college. Shortly afterward, however, nearly all appointments to the civil service were sold publicly at set prices.[9] And in order that the income from this source should be increased, continual changes were being made in the civil service, through the dismissal and reappointment of the civil servants, which implied the collection of the price of their appointments over and over again.[10] One should not forget of course that this state of things, far from being peculiar to Turkey, was in general prevalence all over Europe, and by the end of the sixteenth century the sale of offices at set prices was a regular source of income to meet the requirements of the budget of the Papal court.[11]

At a time, therefore, when the Turkish state had brought to the market all its own civil and ecclesiastical offices, it is not surprising that it was only too eager to turn into good account the shortsightedness of the officials of the Greek Church. And thus the institution of the Patriarchate, which could be of immense value to the national and civic interests of the Greek people under the Turkish rule, was rendered useless almost at its outset by the Greeks themselves.

The history of the Patriarchs after Symeon the Trapezuntine is a long, sad series of humiliations. Symeon himself was not permitted to stay in office for any length of time. The Sultan's Greek stepmother, a certain Mrs. Maro, had a favorite monk of her own whom she wanted to elevate to the Throne of Constantinople. She put therefore two thousand florins on a silver tray and made straight for the Sultan. Needless to say, the silver tray and its contents of gold weighed more than the vote of the Holy Synod, and forthwith Dionysius, Mrs. Maro's favorite monk, succeeded Symeon on the Throne.[12] And the stronger the ambitions of the

Greek clerics grew, the larger the *peshkesh* became and the more frequent the occasions for its collection by the Turks. In 1679 Paul Ricaut wrote: "In former times the Church paid no more to the Great Signor at the change of a Patriarch, than 10,000 Dollars, but the multitude of pretenders for this office hath enhanced the price to 25,000."[13] A few years later Pitton de Tournefort wrote: "This dignity [i.e., the Ecumenical Throne] is being sold to-day for 60,000 dollars."[14] J. Aymon, on the other hand, reports that in 1671, in one and the same year not less than five people— Paissius, Dionysius of Thessalonica, Parthenius, Methodius, and Dionysius of Larissa—sat in succession on the Throne, each having paid the *peshkesh*.[15] It is evident that the Turkish authorities had good reasons for encouraging with all their powers such a state of things, which could only result in the ruin of the Greek Church.

This state of affairs was in itself a sufficient indication that Cyril would not be permitted for long to attend undistracted to the duties of his high office. There were too many petty ambitions at work around him and the Turkish authorities were only too ready to satisfy them. Moreover, a man of Cyril's stature was liable to make things even more difficult for himself by the very contrast of his own personality to that of the mediocrities around him and by the jealousies which that contrast was bound to arouse. And it appears that Cyril did not make any particularly great effort to smooth things down, but let his hand fall heavily on the unworthy and lazy clerics who swarmed in the Patriachate. Aymon says: "The majority of the bishops and the priests, being extremely ignorant and being known as such by all those who were acquainted with them, could not suffer a Patriarch so wise and enlightened as Cyril to preside at their meetings and to address to them rebukes in order to oblige them to attend to their Pastoral duties."[16] Ignorance and superstition were the greatest foes against which Cyril had to fight all through his adventurous career.

Practically no regular schools were in operation at that time among the enslaved Greeks. The nation was being bled white by the terrible system of "child-gathering." Every five years small bands of soldiers visited each little Greek community throughout the empire, provided with a "firman" which gave them the power to carry off all male children over seven years old who were noted for beauty or cleverness. These boys were brought up as Moslems, and to the most promising among them was given every possible opportunity for education. It was from the ranks of these captives that the Turkish Empire got some of its best servants in the highest offices of the state. Thus the blood extracted from the enslaved Greeks was infused into their conquerors to make them stronger.[17] This "tribute of blood" could not but tell very heavily on the spiritual condition of the nation.

Ignorance was particularly conspicuous among the clergy, with very sad effects. The libraries of even those who could read were extremely poor, as their books had to be brought from Venice at great cost.[18] The gross ignorance of the clergy is evidenced by the fact that it affected even the traditional interior decoration of the churches at that time. Tournefort says that when he visited the Levant the pulpit no longer existed in the majority of the churches, not even as a piece of furniture, "for the custom of preaching had been abolished."[19]

We can well imagine how Cyril's blood boiled when he found himself in the midst of such ignorance and realized that he had to rely on the services of a clergy which in its majority was as ignorant and superstitious as the people among whom they were working. Tournefort relates how on one occasion he was given hospitality by an old priest who insisted that he had in his possession a very old prophecy, according to which the Czar of Russia would very soon deliver the Greek nation from the Turkish slavery.[20] The text of the prophecy proved to be nothing more than the names of visitors and some words which they had inscribed on the stones of the nearby ruins of an ancient building, in languages quite unknown to the old priest.[21]

To make things worse for the Greek Church, a Jesuit mission which was in Constantinople at the time of Cyril's arrival had been using very successfully two great weapons—the confessional and education. They only repeated in Constantinople what they had consistently and with great success practiced in other countries of Europe. Lacy Collison-Morley says about them: "In Europe they cemented their power by the control they obtained

both by the confessional and education. . . . Their casuistry has
become a byword. . . . There was no crime they could not and did
not justify, from regicide downwards, for they held that the end
might justify the means."[22] And Ogg affirms the same thing when
he says that among earnest seventeenth-century Catholics there
was a current belief that by the application of casuistry in the
confessional, the Jesuits were teaching a relaxed morality.[23]

It was exactly along these lines that they achieved their great
success in Constantinople. A contemporary of Cyril, Chrysoscule
Logothetis, says about them: "Moreover they had attracted to
themselves many from the common people, i.e. many women and
children, whom they could influence more easily on account of
their sex and age. . . . The women were easily influenced by the
eloquence and the charming manners of these new guides of
conscience, who succeeded in persuading them to come to them
for auricular confession of their sins, without intimidating them
and without imposing any rigorous penance or severe fasting."[24]

But even greater was their success through the school which
they were running in Constantinople for the children of the
Greeks. And this is not to be wondered at, as the Jesuits were
considered to be the best teachers in Europe at that time. G. N.
Clark says: "All Europe admitted at the beginning of the century,
that in educational practice they were supreme. In discipline, in
teaching, in the care of their pupils' health, they were alike successful."[25] "It was through education that they gained their greatest influence in Catholic countries."[26]

With such a creditable past it is no wonder that their school in
Constantinople was a great success from the day it was founded,
especially in view of the almost total lack of any means of education among the Greek population at that time.

While he was still in Alexandria, Cyril followed the progress
of the Jesuit school in Constantinople with great anxiety, as his
letters to his friends testify. He wrote to Uytenbogaert, on the
tenth of October, 1613: "I am the enemy of ignorance. . . . It is
a great disappointment to me that our Pastors and Bishops should
be sunk in the darkness of ignorance. With this I reproach my
countrymen, but without avail. And the Jesuits, grasping the
opportunity, have laid the foundation of a plan for educating

boys at Constantinople, with the same undisputed success as that of a fox amongst poultry."[27] And in a letter to Archbishop Abbot he said: "These emissaries terrify us greatly; reckoning on our simplicity, they use various machinations to bring us under their power, trusting chiefly in their show of erudition and the thorny difficulties of the questions which they themselves raise; while we, meanwhile, labour under a lack of learned men, able to meet these sophists on equal terms."[28]

It is not surprising that these clerical "foxes" were having such a great success among the "poultry" of Constantinople, especially considering the methodical way in which they prepared their "den." One of their good friends, Leo Allatius, describes their college as spacious and furnished with a rich library, where the Greek children were offered education without having to pay any fees.[29] By these means, he says, "they win the favour of the people." "Through these children," says the Jesuit Fleuriau, "we have reconciled many of their parents and even whole families with the Roman Church."[30]

The whole movement was under the protection of the French ambassador in Constantinople, who, acting on instructions given him by his government, more than once used his influence with the Turkish authorities to promote the schemes of his protégés.[31] He did this not so much out of religious conviction as from national motives. The French had secured in the Levant a position of absolute pre-eminence ever since 1536 when Sieur Foret, as the representative of King Francis I of France, had signed a treaty with Sultan Suleiman I, the first of what might be called "modern capitulations," according to which all matters of dispute between Frenchmen and Turks were to be negotiated only in the presence of the French dragoman. They were, moreover, given the right of navigation and commerce upon payment of a tax of five per cent.[32] This was the beginning of the rise of French commerce in the Near East, as all other nations, with the exception of the Venetians, were obliged to conduct their commercial activities in that part of the world under the French flag.[33]

There was a clause in that treaty of 1536 which is of particular interest in our present study. According to this clause the French were granted the right of religious liberty and France was given the right of the protection of the Holy Sites in Palestine, which with the passing of time was interpreted to mean the right of the protection of all Christians living in the Ottoman Empire and generally in the Levant. George Sandys in his *Relation of a Journey*, speaking of his arrival in Alexandria, says, "We lodged in the house of the French consul, unto whose protection all strangers commit themselves."[34]

For some years, however, the French position in the Levant had been deteriorating on account of the increasing influence of the English and later of the Dutch. Both the English and the Dutch endeavored to undermine the privileged position which the French were enjoying in Turkey by representing the religion of the French as idolatrous, thus playing with the well-known feelings of the Moslems against anything savoring of idolatry. In the correspondence on this matter exchanged between Queen Elizabeth and Mourad III, Elizabeth gave herself the title of "The invincible and all-powerful Defender of the true Faith, against the idolaters which distorte the teaching of Christ."[35] And it seems that the agents of Elizabeth were so successful in representing to the Turkish authorities the Protestant faith in its "anti-idolatrous" character as being akin to Islam,[36] that Sinan Pasha, speaking on one occasion to the ambassador of the Emperor of Austria, said: "The only things those English lack in order to be real Moslems is to be circumcised and to pronounce the 'Eshhed' [i.e., the Moslem Confession of Faith]."[37] However that may be, the English signed in 1580 a treaty with the Sultan similar to that which had given the French their privileged position.[38] This was the first blow against French prestige in the Levant. The English were not slow in making the best of their newly acquired rights and contested step by step with the French their privileged position. In 1610, Sandys wrote: "There hath bin some contention betweene him [i.e., the English ambassador] and the French about the protection of the Dutch Merchants, but now they do devide the profits."[39] Very soon, however, this convenient agreement and the sharing of the profits came to an end, as in 1612 Cornelius van Haga, ambassador of the Dutch in Constantinople, and one of Cyril's most faithful friends, signed a treaty of commerce with the Porte, similar to that of the French and the

English, in spite of the opposition of the French ambassador, Breves de Cesy.[40]

Such was the state of the interests of some of the European countries in the Levant at the beginning of the seventeenth century. Cyril's elevation to the See of Constantinople, however, was marked by a decided effort on the part of the French to regain the ground which they had lost to the English and the Dutch. From then on the conduct of French policy passed into the ambitious hands of Cardinal Richelieu, whose never-swerving aim was to check the power both of Spain and of Austria and to build up a position of absolute superiority for France in Europe. Although a Prince of the Church, Richelieu never placed the interests of the Church above those of France. In his instructions to Schomberg, his ambassador to Germany, he wrote: "It is a calumny to say that we are so much under the influence of either Spain or Rome that we should embrace the interests of either to our own prejudice." And further on he says that Huguenots who were loyal to the King should receive the same favor as Catholics.[41] At the time of Cyril's arrival in Constantinople the Thirty Years' War was in progress, and during its course Richelieu had no scruples about making an alliance with the Protestants.[42] To such an extent was his policy in international affairs free of ecclesiastical considerations, that the good Roman Catholic writer, L. F. von Pastor, says in disgust that Richelieu was "an exponent of Machiavellian policy of might, without scruple or regard for right."[43] Thus it happened that in continental Europe the policy of the Cardinal very often clashed with the interests of the Pope.

In Turkey, however, things were different. In his effort to regain for France the position of superiority which it had enjoyed in earlier days, Richelieu found that his chief rivals were two Protestant countries: England and Holland. That was sufficient reason for him to align French policy in the Levant with the schemes of the Roman Church. And thus it came to pass that when Cyril took up his duties as Patriarch of Constantinople he had to reckon not only with the gross ignorance of the majority of the Greek clergy and the petty ambitions of the bishops; not only with the cruel warfare which the Roman Church so resolutely waged against him; but also with the powerful opposition of the French authorities both at home and in the Levant, which saw in the person of Cyril not so much a spiritual leader working hard for the awakening of his people, as an instrument in the hands of Sir Thomas Roe and Cornelius van Haga, the ambassadors of the two powers which contested with France the position of influence. It was unfortunate that so many factors combined to stifle the first breath of Reformation which Cyril had brought to Constantinople.

▣ CHAPTER 7

BEGINNING OF TROUBLE

A s SOON AS Cyril took up his residence in Constantinople he felt the urgent need for measures to neutralize the danger to the Church from the activities of the Jesuits. And in this he was not alone. It seems that there were those, both among the bishops and among the influential laymen, who had not fallen victims to the Roman intrigues, and were at one with Cyril in believing that the activities of the Jesuits should be checked by all means. They did not dare, however, take open action against them, as that would provoke open warfare with the French Embassy, which would be sure to exert all its influence over the Porte and thus cause trouble. They began, therefore, in private conversations and with every possible precaution to warn the people against the Jesuit wiles.[1]

Even this restrained action, however, was too much for the Jesuits, who promptly reacted.[*] According to Chrysoscule

---

[*] It is difficult to state the exact time when troubles began. A. Leger in his *Fragmentum Vitae* says that Cyril had been permitted to attend to his duties without any disturbance for two and a half years.[2] This would bring his first exile to Rhodes as late as the spring or summer of 1624. Philippus Cyprius, on the other hand, reduces the time between Cyril's accession to the throne and his first exile to one year, and thus places his exile toward the end of 1622.[3] This date is corroborated by Father Simon[4] and Le Quien,[5] both of whom place Cyril's first exile in the year 1622. Further proof that Leger's date is untenable are the minutes of a meeting of the *Propaganda Fide* held in Rome on June 27, 1623,[6] from which it appears that the news of Cyril's deposition from the Throne and of his condemnation to exile was already known in Rome. Considering the slow pace at which news traveled at that time—and we shall soon come across another instance when news from Constantinople was very late in reaching the *Propaganda Fide*—it is quite safe to place the exile in Rhodes toward the end of 1622, and the beginning of the trouble which led to it earlier in the same year.

Logothetis, the first trouble broke out in February 1622.[7] The Jesuits, having the support of the French ambassador, attempted to drive Cyril out of his Throne and install in his place another Greek, who would be willing to recognize the rule of the Pope over the whole Church and submit himself to his jurisdiction. It is well attested that they had the open support of the French ambassador even at this early stage. Dom. Alphonse Guepin says that "the presence of this Calvinist on the Patriarchal Throne was a matter of great anxiety for the French court, and both from religious motives as well as for political interests De Cesy, the French ambassador in Constantinople, was keeping him under close observation and doing everything in his power to overthrow him."[8]

It is not quite clear, however, what form this first attempt against Cyril took. It seems more probable that the French ambassador and his missionary friends decided not to appeal to the Porte before they had lost hope of help from the Greek Church itself. They started, therefore, an agitation within the Church. And they had no lack of supporters in this, as there was at that time a growing and influential Romanizing party within the Greek Church. This party had its origin chiefly in the College of St. Athanasius which Pope Gregory XIII had founded in Rome in 1577 for the education of Greek young men.[9] Needless to say, this college was meant to be a means of propaganda, and it proved to be a powerful instrument indeed in the hands of the Roman Church. Peter Arcudios, Leo Allatius, Matthew Caryophylles, Peter Stavrinos, Cannachio Rossi, Athanasius the rhetorician, and Nicephorus Melissinos were only a few of the graduates of this college who, in Cyril's own time, had turned Roman Catholics.[10] All these men spared no efforts in propagating the Roman faith within the Greek Church. And they were very successful, for as a result of their efforts there came into existence within the Church a party of people who, while outwardly retaining their allegiance to the Greek Orthodox Church, were at heart Roman Catholics, ready to bring the Church under the rule of the Pope in accordance with the terms of the Synod of Florence. And thus what only a few years earlier had happened in Poland was repeated in Greece. The extent of the influence of this party can be gathered from the fact that only a few years before Cyril, the See of Constantinople was occupied by Raphael II (1603-1608), a graduate of the College of St. Athanasius,[11] who did everything in his power to promote the Roman plans in the Near East. This party, it appears, convoked a Synod in Constantinople which, after examining the accusations against Cyril as favoring Calvinism, proceeded to depose him.

Thus Allatius expressly says that after Cyril had occupied the Throne for four months, during which he "had been professing the Catholic faith," he began disseminating his heretical ideas, and a Synod was called together to take measures against him.[12] That Cyril began to be widely known at about this time as holding Calvinist views can be seen from a letter of the English ambassador, Sir Thomas Roe, to Archbishop Abbot: "As for the Patriarch himself, I do not doubt but that in opinion of religion he is, as we term him, a pure Calvinist, and so the Jesuits in these parts do brand him."[13]

It is doubtful whether a Synod was really held, as this is attested only by Allatius, Father Simon,[14] and Nicolaos Comnenos Papadopolus[15]—all three fierce enemies of Lucaris—while Le Quien, a Roman Catholic of a more conservative temperament, makes no mention of any Synod's having been assembled. The result of the agitation, however, was the attempt to have Cyril deposed and another man elevated in his place. Chrysoscule Logothetis does not mention the name of this man, but it appears from other sources that he was Gregory of Amassia who, being blind in one eye, was popularly known as "Stravoamassias"—"the blind bishop of Amassia."[16]

When Cyril was confronted with this situation, he immediately took counsel with his friends and it was decided that they should try to keep this affair as strictly as possible within the Church and thus avoid the interference of outsiders. Accordingly, on the following Sunday, Cyril preached in the Cathedral a sermon in which he disclosed to the public the plots that had been made against him, taking care not to mention the Jesuits by name but to allude to them in vague terms, and finally he warned his flock to be on their guard. And then, acting in concert with four archbishops and a large number of clergy, he pronounced the sentence of excommunication against the bishop who had attempted to supplant him, hoping that this display of severity would discourage others who might have similar ambitions.[17]

Far from discouraging the Jesuits, these measures irritated them all the more. The enemies of Cyril saw that they would have to make use of the Turkish authorities in order to have him deposed. As soon as they were able to secure the services of suitable agents, they approached the Grand Vizir. Among those who took an active part in the effort to approach the Turkish authorities, Leger names a certain Archimandrite Euthymius, who had apparently received the promise of Rome that he would succeed Cyril on the Throne.[18] For some reason, however, the promise was not fulfilled and Euthymius was obliged to leave Constantinople and take up his residence in Rome, where we find him after some years offering his counsel to the *Propaganda Fide* in their warfare against Cyril.

A certain Hussein Pasha from Epirus was Grand Vizir at that time, and to him the Jesuits came, supported by the French Embassy, with a double accusation against Cyril: that he was in correspondence with the Great Duke of Russia, and that he incited the inhabitants of one of the islands of the Aegean Sea to rebellion in order to facilitate the occupation of this island by the Florentines. To these accusations the Jesuits added the promise of twenty thousand dollars, should Cyril be expelled from his Throne. This promise in itself would be sufficient for the promotion of the Jesuits' plans, considering the character of Hussein Pasha. It is, however, interesting to note how carefully the Jesuits chose the ground from which to launch their effort to rouse the suspicions of the Turkish authorities against Cyril. At this particular time a war against Poland, which had an unfortunate end for Turkey, had either just been concluded or, more probably, was in its last stages.[19] This had created a very delicate state of affairs so far as Russia was concerned, and eventually led to the deposition and murder of Sultan Osman II. Anyone exchanging letters with important people in Russia at such a time would naturally come under grave suspicion. Cyril admitted that correspondence was indeed exchanged, but added that this was done at the express desire of the Grand Vizir who had preceded Hussein Pasha.

All his protests, however, did not avail to persuade the Vizir of his innocence.

The other accusation against Cyril was equally well selected. The attacks of the Florentines against the Turkish coast and islands during the last thirty years had become a source of increasing annoyance for the Porte.[20] Things were brought to a climax shortly after Cyril's exile, when the Porte was obliged to take the initiative in establishing better relations with Florence.[21] At such a time, therefore, the mere mention of the name of Florence in connection with anyone would be sufficient to place him under the darkest suspicion. Vainly did Cyril protest his innocence. Hussein Pasha was adamant. Forthwith the sentence of Cyril's banishment to the island of Rhodes was pronounced. Both Leger and Smith find it a most fitting divine retribution that before long Hussein Pasha was himself strangled by order of the Sultan in that very cell of the Prison of the Seven Towers in which he had thrown Cyril as a prisoner.[22]

So Cyril was sent to Rhodes, that most beautiful of the islands of the Aegean, "beloved to the Sun and erected above the waves by his powerful influence."[23] He did not stay there long, however, as the situation in Constantinople did not develop as the Jesuits had hoped. Cyril was back in Constantinople by the first of September, 1623.[24]

The Throne, which had been rendered vacant by Cyril's departure, had been filled by the "bishop of one eye," Gregory of Amassia, who was willing to act as an instrument in the hands of the Roman propaganda and who, according to Allatius,[25] if he is to be relied on, had declared publicly his submission to the Roman See by means of letters which he had sent to the Pope. Gregory's tenure of the office was short-lived; it lasted only ten weeks.[26] During this time the Greek population of Constantinople adopted an attitude of passive opposition toward the unexpected occupant of the Throne. They did not recognize him as their pastor, did not attend the services at the Cathedral, did not congratulate him on his "promotion," and, what was worse, they refused to furnish the money on which the Jesuits had counted for the fulfillment of their promise to Hussein Pasha and for the payment of the inevitable *peshkesh*. Thus, as time passed and no solution of the financial problem was in sight, poor Gregory ran the risk of being considered as having defrauded the Turkish treasury and consequently was in danger of being sent to prison.[27] It was not hard, therefore, to persuade him to resign in favor of Anthimus of Adrianople whom the Jesuits put forward as a candidate for the Ecumenical Throne.[28]

Anthimus was not as acceptable a person to the Jesuits as Gregory was. He was a man of no great merits and a person of weak character, but he had one great qualification—he was a man of ample means and could provide the money which the Jesuits so urgently needed for the fulfillment of their promise to the Grand Vizier. So when they appealed to him, he was quite willing to pay for the honor of sitting on the Throne.

He was not, however, much more fortunate than his predecessor. For in the meantime Cyril's friends had succeeded in having him recalled from exile and as soon as the news of his return spread in Constantinople the house in which he was staying was swarmed by friends who came to congratulate him on his safe return. The news was not long in reaching the Patriarchal residence, and terror struck at the heart of old Anthimus when he heard that the lawful pastor of the church was back and that the people had given him such a warm welcome. He at once decided on a plan of action. He made his way secretly to the house where Cyril was staying and offered him his resignation. Cyril did not dare occupy the Throne without first obtaining the permission of the Turkish authorities, but he asked Anthimus to abide by his resignation so that the Throne might be vacant until these authorities would come to a decision concerning his rights to it. This Anthimus promised to do. But at this point things took a most unexpected turn.

As soon as the French ambassador learned of Anthimus' defection he invited him to the Embassy, and there by means of threats and promises of the protection of the Pope and the King of France he persuaded the old man to revoke his resignation. Without delay a procession was formed. The dragomans of the French Embassy—very important people at that time of the "capitulations"—together with a detachment of Janissaries, with Anthimus in their midst, left the French Embassy and made their way slowly toward Galata in order to restore him in his office. By the time they reached the Church of the Patriarchate they had become a large procession and the whole city rang with the news. The hero of this exciting scene, however, was not at all happy with his triumph. His conscience was troubled and his spirit was weighed down with fears. He was aware that he had no rights to the Throne and that he had wronged the lawful pastor of the Church. As soon, therefore, as he could escape the vigilance of the dragomans, who had orders to offer him, even against his will, the protection of the King of France, he came to Cyril by night, cast himself at his mercy, besought and obtained his pardon, and then retired to Mount Athos and spent the remaining days of his life in one of the monasteries there.[29]

It remained now for Cyril to obtain the Grand Vizir's permission to resume his duties, and this was not too difficult to get, provided the *peshkesh* was paid once again. The Greek Church was obliged to do this, and so ended the first round of Cyril's encounters with the Roman Church. Once again he was on the Throne, and although difficulties of a relatively minor importance were not lacking, this time he was permitted to attend to his duties without interruption for a period of eight years.

CHAPTER 8

ROMAN INVASION

T HE SLOW PACE at which news traveled at that time was responsible for a great disappointment which Rome had in connection with its efforts to get rid of Lucaris. Sometime in 1624, De Cesy, the French ambassador in Constantinople, received a letter from the Pope, which he must have read with a sense of bitter irony. "The Roman Church hath heard what thou hast done in Constantinople and praised thy piety. We know what calamities have befallen that son of darkness, that athlete of hell, the pseudo-patriarch Cyril, and that thou hast made every effort to have the venerable Father Anthimus become the leader of the church."[1]

One can imagine the disappointment of the sender of this congratulatory letter, when shortly after its dispatch it was made known in Rome that the "son of darkness, that athlete of hell" had been back in Constantinople for the last year and once again was at the head of the Church, while the "venerable Father Anthimus" was meditating on the vanity of human affairs in the quiet of one of the monasteries of Mount Athos and at a safe distance from the protection of the French ambassador. The bitterness of the disappointment, however, must have spurred Rome to take new measures against Cyril, for soon after the dispatch of the above letter successive waves of activity of Roman origin reached Constantinople. All these waves emanated from the *Congregatio de Propaganda Fide*, which deserves the sad honor of having prosecuted with untiring determination the Roman plans against Cyril to their tragic end.

Foremost among the factors which conspired against Cyril and his work is the fact that his effort for the reformation of the Greek

Church came at a time when the revived *Congregatio de Propaganda Fide* gave a new impetus to the campaign to conquer the Orthodox Orient for the Roman Church.

Pope Gregory XIII, who, as we have seen, was the founder of the College of St. Athanasius in Rome for the education of Greek young men, was also responsible for another measure whose aim was the conversion of the Greek Orient to the Roman faith. This was the founding, in 1573, of a "Congregation for the Dissemination of the Faith" in the East. This was the forerunner of the *Congregatio de Propaganda Fide* which was brought into being by Pope Gregory XV, on the day of Epiphany in 1622, exactly two months after Cyril was elevated to the Throne of Constantinople. Both Gregory XV and Ludovisi, his Secretary of State, had an intimate knowledge of, and sincere admiration for, the centralized organization of the Society of Jesus and endeavored by the creation of the *Congregatio de Propaganda Fide* to place all Roman Catholic missions throughout the world under one central authority, with a view to co-ordinating their activities and securing better results for their labors.[2] Thus it was that the fight against Cyril passed into the hands of the *Congregatio*, which held itself responsible for the contest to the very end. The importance which Rome attached to the fight against Cyril is evident from the fact that, whereas it was stipulated in the chart of the foundation of the *Congregatio* that "only matters of greatest importance were to be brought before the Pope,"[3] yet in more than one instance the Pope himself presided at meetings in which measures against Cyril were to be discussed.

Our sources are not in accord concerning the time when the first measures of the *Congregatio* against Cyril were taken. The older sources, such as Thomas Smith[4] and Chrysoscule Logothetis,[5] place the beginning of hostilities in February 1624. But according to the minutes of the meetings of the *Congregatio* which were published by G. Hofmann, S.J.,[6] these events should be placed a year later. In the meantime reports of the most disquieting nature were coming to the *Propaganda*. Von Pastor mentions that it became known in Rome that Cyril had printed in Wittenberg a catechism written by Zacharias, one of his pupils, with the purpose of spreading Protestant ideas among the Greeks.[7]

Zacharias Gerganos, whom no doubt Von Pastor had in mind, is not known to have been a pupil of Cyril's. He was a contemporary of, but younger than, Cyril. Belonging to a noble family of Epirus, he was taken under the protection of the King of Saxony and studied theology in the University of Wittenberg from 1619 to 1622. While in Wittenberg, he published a new edition of the New Testament. He also prepared a "Christian Catechism" which he published in Wittenberg in 1622.[8] This Catechism, which made its appearance soon after Cyril was elected Patriarch of Constantinople, had definite Protestant tendencies. It seems that Cyril gave it a cordial welcome, as a book useful in his own efforts to reform the Greek Church, and had it circulated in Constantinople. This was probably what gave rise to the rumor that it was Cyril himself who had published the Catechism. At any rate, in his letter of October 1, 1624, to his government in Paris, the French ambassador complained that "numerous Calvinistic Catechisms in script" were circulating in Constantinople through the initiative of the Patriarch.[9]

However this may have been, the *Congregatio de Propaganda Fide* felt very uneasy about Cyril and considered his presence in Constantinople an obstacle to the realization of its own plans. These fears were strengthened in the course of time by letters which Schiattini, who subsequently became Roman Catholic Bishop of Naxos, sent to the *Congregatio* and in which he gave reports of the Calvinistic activities of Cyril in Constantinople.[10] At the outset of its struggle against Cyril the *Propaganda* endeavored to secure the assistance of the Roman Catholic court of Vienna, while at the same time, through letters to the French ambassador, De Cesy, it encouraged him to persevere in his zeal for the Roman faith. It was not satisfied, however, in simply urging the French ambassador to take all possible measures against Cyril, but as soon as it was informed of the return of Cyril to the Throne of Constantinople it wrote a letter to the Apostolic Nuncio in Paris[11] requesting him to ask the King of France to take under his high protection the Patriarchate of Constantinople and to charge his ambassador in Constantinople to bring to bear all his influence in order to have Cyril deposed from the Throne. The

Nuncio was asked to point out to the King that were this Calvinist permitted to pollute Greece with his teaching and ultimately bring about a union of his own Church with "the Calvinist synagogue of the West"—which was the definite aim both of himself and of his Dutch friends—the Catholic Church would be confronted with new enemies. This would create a very serious situation and the Nuncio was asked to do everything in his power to have the King of France take a personal interest in the matter of Lucaris.

In January 1625 the advance guard of the Roman forces arrived in Constantinople in the person of a monk, who was given hospitality at the French Embassy. This monk came from Rome bearing a special message from the *Propaganda Fide* to all the friends of Rome within the Greek Church. The message urged them not to lose courage, as money would not be lacking in their efforts against Lucaris, provided only that they could secure the deposition of Cyril and the elevation in his place of some other bishop about whose friendly attitude to Rome there could be no doubt.[12]

This first movement of Rome was rapidly followed by the dispatch of three different emissaries, all of whom, each in his own way, had as their aim the overthrow of Cyril. First to arrive on the field was Berillus, a certain Greek Jesuit, whose special mission was to submit to the Turkish authorities the accusation that Cyril, through letters and other means, was inciting the Cossacks to take up arms against the Empire. Once again one cannot help admiring the masterly way in which Rome chose its ground against its enemy. The Cossacks, through their incursions on various parts of the Empire, had been for a long time the chief obstacle to the conclusion of peace between Turkey and Russia.[13] Only a year before the arrival of Berillus in Constantinople the Cossacks had attempted their most terrible invasion, when in July 1624 a flotilla of about a hundred and fifty light vessels appeared at the northern entrance of the Bosphorus and retired only after it had laid waste its Asiatic coast.[14] In such a state of affairs any contact with the Cossacks was a crime which could not possibly be expiated; as Thomas Smith puts it, "even if one should offer one's life a thousand times over."[15]

The second emissary, an unnamed layman, came with instructions to prepare the way for a treaty to be concluded between Turkey and Spain,[16] in which case, through the good services of that Catholic state, it would no doubt be easier to secure the assistance of the Turkish authorities against Cyril.

Last but not the least to arrive on the scene was another Greek proselyte of Rome, Cannachio Rossi, a graduate of the College of St. Athanasius, who had instructions to approach Cyril himself with definite proposals from the Holy Father. He was instructed to give Cyril the assurance that the Roman Church always desired peace and union with all Churches, and above all with the Greek Church, which had received in the past the good services of her Catholic sister. And not only in past times, but even more recently, during the Patriarchate of Jeremiah, the Roman Church had done everything in its power to bring about a union with the Greek Church, having spared neither pains nor money for this purpose. A proof of its friendly feelings toward the Greek Church was the founding of a college in Rome for the education of young Greeks, so that a nation so noble and industrious might regain, through piety and education, the place it had held in the past.

As regards more especially the present Patriarch of Constantinople, the Sovereign Pontiff, whose benevolent feelings toward the Greek Church were very strong, would gladly spend large sums of money in order to reunite with the body of the Roman Church one of its most noble members and to give him special financial assistance. But should the rumors which had come from Constantinople prove to be true, the Pope did not see how this union could be effected. He had the information, for example, that the Patriarch rejected the doctrines of the invocation of the saints, the worship and veneration of the images and relics of the saints, the Real Presence of Jesus Christ in the Eucharist, the free will, the authority of the Councils, the traditions, the authority of the Holy Fathers, the need for auricular confession. The Pope was also informed that the Patriarch of Constantinople was sending young men to study in England, where they were being taught these erroneous doctrines, which they were disseminating all over the East. Further, that for this same purpose the Patriarch himself was distributing to the bishops a certain form of Catechism, which he had had printed, and which was full of errors that had been condemned not only by the Apostolic See and the Council

of Trent, but also by his own predecessors; that he had the support of the ambassador of the Huguenots and that he had no
scruples about communicating with them; that he had lifted the
Synodicon and that he no longer knelt before the Holy Eucharist.

The instructions given to Rossi went on to say that the Holy
Father sincerely hoped that all these rumors were without any
foundation and that the Patriarch, as the leader of such a noble
nation, had lived up to the demands of the spiritual and temporal
needs of his people, thus making it possible for the Holy Father
to show him favor and give him, with a good conscience, real and
effective assistance.

If, therefore, these rumors were baseless and the Patriarch was
able to prove to His Holiness that he was innocent, he should so
inform the French ambassador or the ambassador of the Emperor
and give them strong proofs of his innocence. He should also send
to His Holiness through the above ambassadors a Confession of
his faith, in which he should accept the terms of the Council of
Florence and condemn the errors of the Calvinists and the
Lutherans; after which the Holy See would not fail to accord him
its favor and to assist the Church of Constantinople in every
possible way, so that it should regain its proper place among the
Churches dependent on her. His Holiness would impose no other
conditions either on Cyril or on the other Greek bishops save those
which had been decreed by the Council of Florence, provided the
Greek Church condemned and anathematized, as she had done
up to now, the blasphemies of the heretics of the North, such as
the Lutherans and the Calvinists.[17]

Such was the message which Cannachio Rossi was charged to
deliver to Cyril on behalf of the Pope and the *Congregatio de
Propaganda Fide.*

The first consequence of Rossi's arrival in Constantinople was
that the French ambassador De Cesy took offense, as he was
anxious to keep the initiative in the handling of the whole matter
in his own hands. He therefore wrote to Rome and demanded
Rossi's recall. But although the *Congregatio* had decided to leave
the negotiations on this matter in the experienced hands of De
Cesy, it refused to recall Rossi. Thus it was the latter who presented Rome's ultimatum to Cyril.

For indeed this was an ultimatum; Cyril could make no mistake about it. It was easy to see behind the courteous language which, for the time being, was adopted, and the compliments which Rome paid to the "son of darkness, that athlete of hell," that she would be satisfied with nothing less than a complete surrender of Cyril and the Greek Church to Rome. Cyril found himself placed in a difficult position, for he could certainly make no such surrender. On the other hand he knew that his refusal would raise a new tempest against him. He had long deliberations with his friends, especially with the English and Dutch ambassadors, and he finally adopted the course of action which Sir Thomas Roe suggested to him, namely, to give no answer to the Roman proposals, inasmuch as these were not made in writing.[18]

This attitude of prudence highly displeased the Jesuits, who, realizing that they could hope for nothing from Cyril himself, resorted once again to violence against him. Once again they made use of the Latinizing party within the Church, which they tried to persuade, by means of a promise of twenty thousand dollars, to take action against Cyril with a view to overthrowing him and replacing him by one of their own number.

The horizon began to darken again. The charge which had been made against Cyril in connection with the Cossacks, together with the possibility of a promise of a new *peshkesh* to the Turks, forboded no good for Cyril. He therefore retired to his own house, avoiding all public appearances, while his good friends, the English and Dutch ambassadors, approached the Turkish authorities, revealed to them the sinister plans of the Roman emissaries against Cyril, and thus cleared the situation. But it would be against the Turks' own nature to be persuaded of Cyril's innocence, however obvious that may have been, without the assistance of bribery. The ambassadors, therefore, sealed their arguments by the offer of a sum of ten thousand dollars, which helped persuade the Turkish authorities that Cyril was quite innocent of the charges made against him. This gave Cyril and his Church a respite before the next Roman wave reached the shores of Constantinople.

And Cyril made good use of this respite. He saw that there could be no hope of the Greek Church resisting the attacks of Rome so long as ignorance about the great Christian doctrines

prevailed among the Greek people and especially among the
clergy. He invited therefore various learned men to come and
settle in Constantinople and help him in his work.[19] Chief of
these was Theophilus Corydalleus. About this time a school had
been founded in Constantinople in connection with the Patriarchate, whose purpose was to react against the school of the
Jesuits. Very much depended, of course, on the man who would
be in charge of this school, and Cyril gave one more evidence of
his theological status of that time by his choice of the person for
that responsible office. He asked the famous Theophilus Corydalleus, who was at that time headmaster of a school in the island
of Zante, to come and take charge of the school in Constantinople.
Corydalleus was famous for his erudition—he had studied, like
Cyril himself, in Padua under the same teacher, Cremonini, and
this may have been one reason for Cyril's deciding in his favor.
The strongest reason, however, which must have influenced Cyril
in his choice was that Corydalleus was also famous for his in-
disputable Calvinist views in matters of theology.[20] With Corydalleus, therefore, in Constantinople, Cyril could feel sure that
the education of the young in this city was in the hands of a man
who held the same beliefs as he did, and shared with him the
desire to see the Greek Church reformed.

CHAPTER 9

THE CONGREGATIO IN RAGE

IN ONE OF THE TWO NICHES which are on either side of the altar of the apse of St. Peter's Cathedral in Rome stands a beautiful statue made by the great Bernini. The statue represents a man with a long square-cut beard, the *bella barba*, a big forehead and thick brows, under which shine two eyes full of pride and power.[1] It is the statue of Pope Urban VIII of the House of Barberini whose emblem has the bees carved on its robe. They are also reminders of the bountiful way in which Pope Urban VIII had provided for his kinsmen at the expense of the public funds, giving rise to the saying: *Quam bene pavit apes, tam male pavit oves*— "As he has fed his bees well, so has he fed his sheep badly."[2]

It is commonly acknowledged that Urban VIII was the greatest Pope of the seventeenth century.[3] And he was fully conscious of his merits. "I do not know of any other Pope in whom this self-confidence attained so high a degree." "Self-reliant and self-willed, he kept the management of affairs strictly in his own hands." With these words two historians, a Protestant and a Roman Catholic respectively, expressed their opinion of him.[4] A character like his would naturally tend to be intolerant and impatient with others; and such Urban VIII was. Even his death was caused by his distress when forced to sign a humiliating peace with the Duke of Parma. And he died invoking heaven's vengeance on his enemies, who had humiliated him on the battlefield.[5]

Urban was not particularly noted for his piety. An acquaintance who knew him when he was still a cardinal described his cynicism well when he wrote to Galileo, who was condemned during Urban's pontificate: "Cardinal Barberini told me last night that the affairs of the heavens are of little account here below."[6] When he was a nuncio in Paris he showed a great interest in the Roman Catholics in England; so the Pope appointed him Protector of Scotland. As he was also greatly interested in the Greeks—being a Greek scholar—Gregory XV named him Protector of the Greek College, making him a member of the *Propaganda*.[7] On his elevation to the See, he was ex officio responsible for the progress of the work of this body, and so the case of Cyril passed into his able, impatient, and cruel hands. Concerning this affair he repeatedly evinced a keen interest and directed personally the efforts of the *Congregatio* to get rid of this very undesirable occupant of the See of Constantinople. That he would have no scruples about causing the death of Cyril is shown by the feelings he expressed when the news of the death of another undesirable contemporary, Gustavus Adolphus, King of Sweden, reached Rome. "The Pope has learnt with joy," writes his nephew Cardinal Francis Barberini, "the disappearance of that serpent. . . . His satisfaction is beyond words."[8]

Well might Urban VIII get impatient with the news that came from Constantinople. Not only had the triple plot so carefully prepared against Cyril come to nothing, but that "son of darkness" had the audacity to appoint as the head of his school in Constantinople such a well-known Calvinist as Corydalleus. This exasperated both Urban and the *Congregatio*[9] and obliged them to take new measures against Cyril immediately.

A meeting of the *Propaganda* was accordingly held on November 13, 1627, at the palace of its prefect, Cardinal Bandini. Bandini was one of the ablest members of the Sacred College, a man famous for his political experience and efficiency, considered by many as the future Pope even while Gregory XV was still living.[10] In the capable hands of this man lay the direction of the affairs of the *Propaganda* and of the war which Rome waged against Cyril. Present at the above-mentioned meeting were, besides the prefect of the *Propaganda*, Cardinals Millini, Ludovisi, Megalotti, and Barberini (the Pope's nephew).[11]

During this meeting letters were read from the French ambassador in Constantinople, as well as from the Greek Archbishop of Naxos, Jeremias Barbarigo, to the effect that Cyril lost no time in spreading the Calvinist doctrines among the Greeks. In this effort he had the support of the English and Dutch ambassadors, and was regarded favorably even by the representative of Venice. De Cesy explains this favor shown to Lucaris by Venice by the fact that the Venetian interests in the Ottoman Empire at that time clashed with those of Rome.[12]

It was imperative, therefore, that new measures should be taken against Cyril if the Greek Church was to be prevented from being won over by the Reformation. Accordingly the following decisions were taken:

(1) That the Greek Jesuit Father Stavrinos should be asked to send to the *Propaganda* a book which Andrew Eudaemon, a fellow countryman of his and a member of the Society of Jesus, had written in refutation of the Catechism of Zacharias Gerganos. Already in April 1624 the *Propaganda* had ordered the printing of this book.[13] Dr. Peter Arcudios and the Greek Archbishop Caryophylles, who were friendly toward Rome, were to censor it before it was put in circulation. It seems, however, that Caryophylles was not altogether satisfied with the book, for he prepared his own refutation of the Catechism of Gerganos, which was published four years later by the *Propaganda* itself.[14]

(2) That the famous letter in which the Greek Cardinal Bessarion, an old proselyte of Rome, gave his reasons for joining the Church of Rome, should be printed and widely circulated in Greece.

(3) That measures should be taken to expose Cyril in public as a preacher of Calvinism.

(4) That the French ambassador should use the name and authority of his King to bring about the deposition of Cyril. For this purpose money should not be spared, although it would be better to reserve available funds for a literary campaign against Cyril.

(5) That the Apostolic Nuncio in Paris should use all his influence with the King of France to secure the latter's personal interest in these plans. The French King should be made to see the great danger which would arise out of a possible alliance between the schismatic Greeks and the English, Dutch, and German Protestants. It does not seem, however, that such exhortations were necessary in the French court, because King Louis XIII had

already shown a personal interest in the "affair Lucaris," as can be judged by the correspondence on this matter between De Cesy and his master. On April 15, 1623, he wrote to the King: "Ever since your majesty instructed me to bring about, if possible, the deposition of the Greek Patriarch of Constantinople, my time has not been wasted, and if nothing untoward arises, I hope to overwhelm him, although he has very strong support." Exactly one month later Louis XIII wrote from the palace in Fontainebleau to his ambassador in Constantinople: "I have already written to demand that you endeavor to have the Patriarch of Constantinople deposed from his office, because he is a Huguenot and tainted with heresy. And as it is of great importance to the Catholic religion that the one who holds this office should be a person of moral living, professing the true religion, I shall be greatly pleased if you succeed in having the Patriarch deposed, and someone else put in his place. Advise me at your earliest convenience concerning the results of your endeavors." This letter, however, crossed another written by De Cesy to the King. "Since I wrote my last letter to Your Majesty, I have accomplished what you ordered me to do. I have handled the case of the deposition of the Greek Patriarch of Constantinople, in such a way as to have him removed from his throne by order of the Grand Vizir. His successor, a good old man, an ex-archbishop of Amassia of Pontus, has just come to thank me."[15]

(6) "The Greek merchants should take a definite stand against Lucaris, if they do not want to forfeit the protection of the Christians." This is the wording used by the Roman Catholic historian Von Pastor.[16] The actual decision of the *Propaganda*, however, as preserved in the minutes of its meeting, is much stronger. It threatened the Greek merchants that unless they took a definite attitude against Cyril, they "would suffer injuries from the Christian soldiers."[17] These "Christian soldiers" were pirates, who at that time in great numbers and under various flags were carrying on plundering and slave-hunting raids all over the Mediterranean Sea.[18] Still fresh in the minds of the Greek merchants was the memory of previous raids against them by the Maltese pirates whom the Holy See had ordered "not to spare the heretical Greeks," at a time when the rival claims of the Roman

and the Greek Orthodox Churches on the guardianship of the Holy Sepulcher at Jerusalem were being examined by the Porte.[19] The *Propaganda* was now threatening the Greeks with a new outbreak of hostilities by these noble "Christian soldiers," unless they declared themselves openly as enemies of Cyril.

Such were the decisions taken at that meeting of the *Propaganda*. In the meantime, another measure was put into practice which had been decided upon at an earlier time. This measure came at a time when Cyril and the Greeks of Constantinople had begun to hope that they were going to enjoy a period of peace.[20] In December 1626, Rome sent an "Anti-patriarch" to the Levant, not "in order to supplant the Patriarch," as Allatius puts it, but "in order to supervise the interests of the Roman Catholic Church in the Near East, and prevent the poison of the heretics from corrupting its own members, as it had a number of Greeks."[21] The Anti-patriarch was given the authority of the Pope to "build and destroy, to plant and uproot, and do anything that would promote the plans of Rome."[22] He was also accompanied by a treasurer, who had in his keeping the money with which the *Propaganda* had decided to finance the "affair Lucaris."

The presence of this treasurer renewed the bitterness which the arrival of Cannachio Rossi had roused in the French ambassador, because he was anxious to keep in his own hands both the initiative in the struggle against Cyril and the handling of the money intended for this cause, for reasons not unrelated to the fact that he was notorious for his debts.[23] It seems, however, that the *Congregatio* had its own reasons for not wanting to leave the money in the hands of De Cesy, as the English ambassador wrote at this time: "Saint Peter does not trust the French Ambassador with His money." The presence of a treasurer by the side of the Apostolic Suffragan was meant to add to the prestige of the office of the latter the glitter of gold which at that time had a special charm both for the Greeks and for the Turks of the Levant. Moreover, the Anti-patriarch had the authority to establish Roman Catholic bishops in Smyrna and in certain islands of the Aegean. These, by their education so manifestly superior to that of the Greek Orthodox bishops, were certain to impress the Greeks favorably and thus increase the confusion existing within large sections of the Greek Church at that time.

Toward the end of 1626 this Suffragan arrived in the island of Naxos, to which island the French ambassador immediately dispatched a bishop and two Jesuits to enhance the splendor of the welcome which was extended to this envoy of the Pope. This delegation from Constantinople conducted the Suffragan to the island of Chios, where a magnificent welcome awaited him, and intended to bring him from Chios to Constantinople itself. The arrogance and vanity of this man, however, defeated his own plans. For in the places which he visited the envoy was so highhanded in his dealings, not only with the Greeks but also with the Roman Catholics who did not belong to the Jesuit party, that a general outcry rose against him—on the part of the Greeks, because they saw in the arrival and proceedings of this emissary of the Pope a new danger to their religious freedom; and on the part of the Roman Catholics who were not in sympathy with the Jesuits, because they feared lest this man's arrogance would provoke the displeasure of the Turkish authorities against them all indiscriminately.

So, another attempt on the part of Rome to penetrate into the Greek Orient came to an inglorious end. How did this come about? It is not easy to say. It appears that Cyril's powerful friends had intervened with the Turkish authorities. Beyond this, however, we know very little about the form which the reaction against the Suffragan took. But all of a sudden, the scenery underwent a radical change. The pompous procession of the Suffragan and his retinue was cut short; the titulary bishops sent from Rome, together with some of their Jesuit friends, were cast into prison; their official papers were seized; and the Apostolic Suffragan was saved from the humiliation of a Turkish prison only by the haste with which he exchanged the field of his short-lived triumphs for the safety of Rome. This unexpected calamity which befell the Jesuits of Constantinople is in some way connected with another episode in Cyril's adventurous career.

CHAPTER 10

THE PRINTING HOUSE
IN CONSTANTINOPLE

IN JUNE 1627 an English ship sailed into the harbor of Constantinople and brought to Cyril and his work reinforcements of a most desirable nature. Among its passengers was a Greek monk by the name of Nicodemus Metaxas. Metaxas was a well-educated man. He had received his education chiefly from his uncle, another Nicodemus Metaxas, bishop of the island of Cephallonia, with whom he shared a great love for their enslaved country and a desire to bring the lights of education to their fellow countrymen. Later the younger Nicodemus was to succeed his uncle in the See of Cephallonia.

When his education was completed, Nicodemus Metaxas went to London in 1620, and settled there with his brother who was a merchant. He saw clearly that books were the great and most urgent need of his people, and this need he resolved to satisfy in some measure. So, with his brother's financial help, he set up in London a small Greek printing house, which published some useful Greek books. With the passing of time, however, Metaxas realized that London was too far from Greece to be a suitable place for a Greek printing house. In due time, therefore, he decided to transfer his field of operations from London to Constantinople. That is how we find him landing in Constantinople in June 1627.

The ship which brought Nicodemus Metaxas to Constantinople carried in its hold a number of large cases which contained the entire equipment of the former printing house of London, together with a fine collection of books. And now the problem which had puzzled the mind of their owner ever since the ship cast anchor, was how to get them through customs without arousing the suspicions of the Turkish authorities, whose ignorance in such matters would only tend to make them more suspicious.

As soon, therefore, as Metaxas landed, he went straight to the Patriarchate to ask for the assistance of the Patriarch, about whom he had heard in London from his friend Metrophanes Critopoulos. It is not difficult to imagine the joy of Lucaris at the news that close by, in the very harbor of the city, lay the means of establishing the first printing house among the enslaved Greek people, which would help him to disseminate far and wide among his fellow countrymen the great truths which he loved and for which he was fighting.[1]

Great as his joy was, however, he realized that the printing house was not yet within his reach and that to pass those cases through the suspicious customs authorities was too big an undertaking for him alone. So he asked the Archbishop of Corinth to accompany Metaxas to the English ambassador and to appeal to him on Cyril's behalf for his assistance in this very important matter.

At first the English ambassador hesitated to get involved in an undertaking which was fraught with danger. But he did not want to refuse his services to his friend the Patriarch in connection with such a fine project. So after a series of consultations with Cyril, with the Patriarch of Alexandria, Gerassimus Spartaliotes, and with the Dutch ambassador, the English ambassador secured an interview with the Grand Vizir, from whom he obtained without much difficulty the permission to have the precious cargo unloaded.

Cyril was not without fears concerning the possible reaction of the Jesuits and their powerful friends against a printing house operating under his control. He therefore expressed the desire that the printing press be set up in the Embassy itself. But Sir Thomas Roe, feeling that he would be carrying too far his protection of Lucaris if he were to turn part of the Embassy into a Greek printing house, refused this request. He hired, however, a house in which the printing press was established. The house was near the English Embassy, but it was even nearer the French

Embassy and it was from this quarter that Metaxas and his friends were now to expect trouble.[2]

That the Jesuits would be enraged at this new move of their adversary was to be expected. But what would be sure to make them even angrier was the fact that the *Congregatio de Propaganda Fide* had at that particular time set up a Greek printing house in Rome. In 1622 it was decided that a printing press, provided with Greek, Latin, Arabic, Armenian, and Illyrian type, should be placed at the disposal of the *Propaganda*. Part of the equipment was given by the Vatican library, and the press was finally set up on July 14, 1626; that is, only eleven months before the arrival of Metaxas in Constantinople.[3] The authorities of the *Propaganda* and their Jesuit agents in Constantinople had, no doubt, great hopes that their press would help inundate the Near East with their literature. And it was with feelings of dismay that they saw at this time a rival printing press being established in Constantinople, which, so far as their work among the Greeks was concerned, would counteract their activities in some measure. They decided, therefore, to try by all possible means to snatch this powerful weapon out of Cyril's hands. And so, only a few months after Metaxas landed in Constantinople we find the *Propaganda* in session on November 13, 1627, to discuss measures to be taken against Lucaris. One of these was to try by every means to persuade the Turks to forbid the operation of the Greek printing house in Constantinople.

At first the Jesuits made use of flattery and cunning. They conceived the plan of attracting Metaxas to their own side and sent him courteous invitations to visit them in their monastery. They insinuated that by joining them he would clear himself of the stain attached to him by the fact that he had studied in England. Metaxas did not seem very eager to have his good name cleared of the stain, and so he turned a deaf ear to the polite invitations of the Jesuits. Realizing, however, that his adversaries would before long employ more drastic methods he gave himself wholeheartedly to making the best of his opportunity.

As soon as the printing press was established, he started work, and it is amazing to see the number of books he was able to publish in the short time that his printing press was permitted to operate. And the nature of all the books published was such as to make it clear to the Jesuits that Cyril and Metaxas were serious in their intentions. Among the first books to be printed was one by Meletios Pegas, in which that celebrated uncle of Cyril, in a series of letters, examined and repudiated the claim of the Pope to be the head of the whole Church. Once again the nephew showed due respect for the work of his great uncle. This was followed by another book on the same subject written by Nilus, Archbishop of Thessalonica. And still another one, on the same subject, appeared shortly afterward written by Gabriel, Archbishop of Philadelphia. Other books followed on various controversial themes, such as the one on purgatory by Barlaam.[4] Strange to say, the most innocuous of all the books published by the Greek printing house of Constantinople was a short treatise on the Jews by Cyril himself. Not that this indicated any change of tactics on his part. On the contrary, at this very time he was at work preparing his big assault, in the form of a Catechism in which he stated the position of the Greek Church and his own on the various articles of the Christian faith, as against the position taken by the Church of Rome. This Catechism, or Confession of Faith, was intended to be Cyril's great contribution to the issue which was dividing the East from the West, and was to be printed in the printing house of Metaxas. Some historians assert that the famous *Confession of Faith* by Lucaris is indeed among the books which came out of the printing press of Metaxas.[5] But this is rather improbable. Legrand, that great authority on Greek texts of the sixteenth and seventeenth centuries,[6] examined this matter carefully and came to the conclusion that these historians were misled by the title of the first edition of the Confession, in which it is stated that it was "written in Constantinople in March 1629," to assume that it had been printed there. On the other hand the thorough examination which Legrand made of the paper and the type used in the first edition produced no evidence of the place where it had been printed. To Legrand's comments we may add that in March 1629, when the first edition of the Confession was printed, the printing house of Constantinople was, according to the historical data in our possession, a thing of the past. We may only state with certainty that Lucaris intended to have his Confession printed in Metaxas' printing house. But the Jesuits forestalled him.

When these saw that words of flattery had no effect on Metaxas, they immediately changed their tactics and attempted to intimidate him by threats. They hinted that they would have him assassinated some night when he was returning to his lodgings, or even in his own room while he slept. Metaxas realized that the situation was getting serious, so he appealed once again to his patron, the English ambassador, Sir Thomas Roe, who added to the many kindnesses shown to Cyril and to his work yet another by offering to Metaxas a room in the Embassy where he would be safe.

The only way now open to the Jesuits, in their efforts to have the work of the printing press stopped, was by making use of the Turks, and this they did. This time Cyril himself opened the way for them by that innocent book which he had written on the Jews. This the Jesuits examined carefully and discovered in it, to their great joy, one or two passages in which Cyril criticized mildly certain beliefs of the Moslems. With this book in their hands, making use of the mediating services of an ex-Voyvode of Galata who was on friendly terms with the Grand Vizir, they were able to present their accusations against Cyril and Metaxas. These were that Cyril had insulted the Koran through his books and that Metaxas, being a man well acquainted with the art of war, had come to Constantinople with the specific purpose of stirring the people to sedition against the Turkish authorities and had used his strange machinery to falsify the official documents of the Sultan and thus create confusion within the Empire.

The Grand Vizir was deeply impressed by these accusations and decided to take immediate measures against Metaxas and his printing activities. He therefore commanded an officer of the army to take a company of Janissaries and proceed to the printing house in order to seize Metaxas and collect proofs of his crime. These Janissaries were an army corps famous for their ferocity and composed of renegade Greeks, the sad fruit of the system of "child-gathering."

It was the fourth of January 1628. Hardly six months had elapsed since Metaxas had landed in Constantinople, where he had developed such admirable activity in so short a time. The company of the Janissaries were ready to carry out the orders which they had received. But the French ambassador, who apparently had a taste for the dramatic element, managed to have the execution of the order postponed for two days. He had the information that the English ambassador had invited to dinner on the sixth of January, day of the Epiphany, a number of people among whom were the Patriarch and the Representative of Venice. And he planned to have these two events coincide, so that, as he put it himself, he should "add some sauce to the dishes" of the ambassadorial dinner.[7]

So at midday of the sixth of January, when Sir Thomas Roe's guests were enjoying the bounty of his table, a company of Janissaries invaded the house of Metaxas, after blockading all the streets that led to it, lest the culprit escape them. The sight of the dreaded Janissaries, and of the special measures of precaution taken, spread panic through that whole quarter of the town. No one, however, knew the reason for all this commotion.

It so happened that at the time of the visit of the Turkish officer and his soldiers, Metaxas was not in the printing house. He was just returning from the Church of Galata, in the company of the secretary of the English ambassador. Some people from the crowd recognized him and pointed him out to the officer as the man for whom he was searching. The officer, however, did not believe them, or at any rate did not dare seize Metaxas, whom he saw dressed in an English-made suit and hat and not in the usual attire of the Greeks of Constantinople. And when the ambassador's secretary assured the officer that the person wearing the English suit and hat was in his master's service, all doubts were dispelled and Metaxas was allowed to go on. In this strange way an English-made suit probably saved the life of a man useful to the Greek nation at that critical time.

It saved Metaxas, but not his property. The captain, enraged at finding that the man for whom he had come had slipped through his hands, let his soldiers loose to plunder and destroy to their heart's content. And it is known from contemporary history that nothing short of total destruction would be likely to satisfy a Janissary's heart. They broke open chests of drawers and cupboards in their search for proofs of Metaxas' guilt. The books and those pieces of furniture and machinery which they could not take away with them, they destroyed.

The grievous news at last reached the English Embassy. The ambassador felt that this was a personal insult against him and against his royal master, since it was he who had secured the permission of the authorities to have the printing press set up and the house in which it was established had been hired in his own name. It was clear to him that he should have to take very drastic measures in order to re-establish his prestige which had so badly suffered.

In the meantime Cyril's book on the Jews was being examined by a number of mullahs, or provincial judges, in the presence of the Grand Vizir. And as they examined it more carefully it seemed less and less clear to them that it contained the blasphemies against the Koran which the Jesuits had attributed to it. The case was at last submitted to the higher authority of the Mufti, who pronounced his judgment on it by saying that "All doctrine contrary to the precepts of Mohamet is not necessarily a blasphemy or a crime. That since the christians had secured the Imperial permission to profess their doctrines, it was no more criminal for them to do this by printing their beliefs than it was by preaching them. And in accordance with the law it was not the diversity of opinion that was punishable, but the scandal which might accompany its propagation." A judgment so liberal, sober, and broadminded as this, coming from the lips of a Moslem, was like a resounding slap in the face of those Christian missionaries who went so far as to make themselves defenders of the prestige of the Koran in order to find weapons with which to fight a fellow Christian.

This judgment of the Mufti shook considerably the Grand Vizir's conviction about the guilt of Metaxas and made him begin to doubt the wisdom of the course he had adopted in sending that company of Janissaries and of the summary way in which they had dealt with the situation.

At this point the English ambassador appeared on the scene. For two days following the events he had kept himself in his Embassy, and on the third day he sought and secured an audience with the Grand Vizir. In a very frank and quite outspoken way he reminded the Grand Vizir that it was by his own permission that the printing house had been set up, and that nothing had been done in this connection without his approval or his knowledge. The English ambassador, therefore, was greatly surprised to see that the Grand Vizir had suddenly developed such grave suspicions against his friends and had allowed such outrages to be committed against them.

The Grand Vizir, who had a great regard for the English ambassador, protested that he did not have the least intention of insulting him, and that he was amazed at the impudence of those who had deceived him with their false accusations against Metaxas. The ambassador was not, however, to be appeased, but seeing that he had already won the first round with the Grand Vizir, he redoubled his protests and declared that he would not be satisfied unless the criminals who had engineered this plot against Metaxas were punished in an exemplary way and that full reparation was made to him for the damage which he had suffered.

In the meantime the Patriarch, who had kept to his house for the fear of more outrages, received a visitor. The visitor was Cannachio Rossi, the special emissary of the Pope, who was still lingering in Constantinople. Rossi was not aware of the latest developments in the situation; he only knew of the Roman triumph against Metaxas, and had come to make the bitter cup which the Patriarch had just drunk even more bitter by his own personal insults. Rossi's cheap triumph, however, did not last long. The protests of the ambassador prevailed with the Grand Vizir, who issued an order that Cannachio Rossi and the Jesuits who had so falsely accused Metaxas should be cast into prison.

The situation had by now undergone a complete change. The triumphant Jesuits and Cannachio Rossi, panic-stricken, confined themselves to their monastery, not daring to appear in public. In spite of all these precautions three Jesuits were seized and cast into prison, and shortly afterward Cannachio Rossi followed them. In the meantime the French ambassador, who realized bitterly that it was he himself who would be obliged to taste the "sauce" destined for his English colleague's dinner, made use of all possible means, from flattery to threats, with the Turkish authorities, in order to have his protégés released. But all his efforts remained fruitless. He sought an audience with the Grand Vizir, which was denied him. At last the Caimacam, the Grand Vizir's deputy, said to him: "If you wish to remain here and behave as an ambassador should, you will always be welcome and will be given the respect due to the dignity of your office. But if you think that you have the right to protect the enemies of the Porte, and that your King's friendship for the Porte means nothing more than this, you are free to leave this country, whenever you please. We shall take good care to inform your King about the real state of affairs, so that full justice should be done both to him and to the Porte."[8] This was very plain speaking, which the French ambassador could not fail to understand.

At last, after much deliberation, an order was issued that the Jesuits should be deported from all territories of the Ottoman Empire. This was immediately communicated to the authorities of Chios, Smyrna, Aleppo, and Cyprus, in order that the decision of the Porte might take effect against any Jesuits residing there. The three Jesuits who had been seized in Constantinople were put on a ship and, after a few unsuccessful attempts on their part to escape, were safely deposited on Italian soil early in 1628.[9]

The satisfaction felt by the Greek Church in Constantinople and her friends was best expressed by Sir Thomas Roe: "They are ready to burst with chagrin at being thrown out. I hope that hereafter they will trouble as little as possible the poore Greek Church to whom their practices have cost twelve thousand dollars, to say nothing of this last insurrection against the authority and the life of the Patriarch and against my honour."[10]

That "hereafter they will trouble as little as possible the poore Greek Church" was probably too bold a wish to be expressed by one who knew the tenacity and cunning with which the Society of Jesus promoted its plans. No sooner had the banished Jesuits arrived in Italy than they made every endeavor to have the order of their banishment recalled so that they might return to Constantinople. As the French ambassador was *persona non grata* with the Turks at that time, the Austrian ambassador, Baron von Kuefstein, was appealed to and he made all possible effort to have the order of banishment revoked. In pursuing this object, he made use of means hardly compatible with the dignity of the ambassador of a great power, such as the subtle interpretation which he suggested to Article 7 of the Treaty of Vienna. This article provided religious freedom for all Christians in Turkey. (The Turkish term for "Christians" was "Issevi" which meant "followers of Jesus.") Baron von Kuefstein seized upon the term "Issevi" and suggested that the "followers of Jesus," for whom religious liberty was provided by the Treaty of Vienna were none other than the members of the "Society of Jesus." This argument, however, was altogether too clever to be effective, and Von Kuefstein had to give up his efforts.[11] It was De Cesy who eventually opened once again the way to Constantinople for his protégés.

It has been said that "when you chase a Jesuit out through the door, he comes back through the window,"[12] and it was through the window that they came back to Constantinople. When the storm had abated and the first impressions had been forgotten, the French ambassador secured permission for two Jesuits to come to Constantinople and act as chaplains of the Embassy.[13] It need hardly be said that these two Jesuits did not confine themselves to what would normally be considered as the duties of a chaplain. In the course of time more "chaplains" were imported for the Embassy, and thus the Society of Jesus was re-established in Constantinople in spite of the disgrace it had suffered after the episode of Metaxas.

Nevertheless the hope which Sir Thomas Roe expressed that "hereafter they will trouble as little as possible the poore Greek Church" came true, for from this point the Jesuits disappear almost completely from the life and work of Lucaris. Not that Rome withdrew her thumb from the Greek pie, or that Lucaris was allowed to proceed undisturbed with his work of reformation in the Greek Church. Quite the contrary. After the humiliation which Rome suffered in connection with the episode of Metaxas, the *Propaganda* took up again with redoubled zeal its efforts to get rid of the Calvinist Patriarch. It dispensed, however, with the services of the Jesuits. Another monastic order proffered itself as an instrument for the promotion of the plans of the *Propaganda*. At this stage the center of gravity of the effort of the

Church of Rome to check the Reformation movement in the
Greek Orient shifted from the Jesuits to the Capuchins, and from
the ambassador of France, De Cesy, to the ambassador of the
Emperor, Rudolph Schmidt Schwarzenhorn. Of this, however,
we shall speak in fuller detail in a following chapter.

Before taking leave of Metaxas, let us see what became of his
printing press. In his *History of the Patriarchs of Jerusalem*,[14]
Dositheus says that during the troubles that broke out "the press
was cast into the sea." Legrand, however, states that this is not
true and that Metaxas was still in possession of his printing press
when he became Archbishop of Cephallonia.[15] However that may
be, the printing house of Constantinople never resumed its activities, either because Metaxas was disappointed or because his
equipment had suffered irreparable damages at the hands of the
Janissaries. This was the end of a beautiful dream.

One can only imagine the wrath of the *Propaganda* when the
news of the disaster which befell the Jesuits of Constantinople
was known. No time was lost before new measures against the
hated Patriarch were taken. A meeting of the *Congregatio* was
convened for the twenty-first of July 1628 in the palace of Cardinal Bandini. In this meeting letters received from De Cesy were
read, and then it was decided: That all Roman missionaries in
Constantinople should try to secure the assistance of the Patriarchs of Alexandria, Antioch, and Jerusalem in their efforts against
Lucaris; that the advice of the Greek bishops who were friendly
toward Rome should be asked concerning the best way to establish legal proceedings against Lucaris; that the Nuncio in Venice
should enlighten the Venetian Senate with regard to the theological ideas of Lucaris and put an end to the support which the
Venetian Representative had been giving him; that eighteen
thousand dollars should be sent to Constantinople, twelve thousand of which would be contributed by the Holy See and the
remaining six thousand by the Most Christian King of France, to
be used in the fight against Cyril, with the clear understanding
that this money would be given to the Greek bishops only after
they had secured Cyril's deposition; that Père Joseph of Paris,
head of the Capuchins, should be asked to proceed to Constan-

tinople, under the pretext of visiting the missionaries of his order there, while in reality his mission would be to promote the deposition of Lucaris.[16]

Père Joseph was Joseph Leclerc du Tramblays, the famous "Grey Eminence," Richelieu's close friend and right hand in the direction of the intricate foreign policy of France at that time. Richelieu did not grant his friend permission to accept the invitation of the *Propaganda*, as he could not be spared from the Foreign Office in Paris at that time.[17] But after that, Père Joseph took a personal interest in the matter of Lucaris, and most of the measures subsequently taken against the Patriarch were first submitted to his approval.

Of all the strange personalities of the seventeenth century Father Joseph was possibly the strangest; he was a mixture of religiosity, mysticism, and political cunning, about whom a colleague in the French Foreign Office had said: "The Father had in reality no soul, but in its stead were holes and quicksands, to which every one who attempted to have dealings with him needs must fall."[18] Father Joseph had also some personal interest in Greece. One of his dreams was to organize a crusade against the Turks and have Constantinople liberated and the Byzantine Empire revived—under French tutelage, of course. For this purpose he gave his support to the Duke of Nevers, whose paternal grandmother was a descendant of the imperial family of the Palaeologi. In order to promote the case of the crusade he visited Rome and Spain and on his way he composed a long lyrical rhapsody on the liberation of the Greeks from Turkish bondage. In his poem he addresses himself to Hellas and says: "If in order to succour thee, I overturn the world, it is all too little for my wishes: to quench the fires of my ardour, I must drown me in a sea of blood."[19] It is small wonder that to such a man the case of Lucaris presented a special interest and that "the fires of his ardour" were unquenchable.

A further meeting of the *Congregatio* was called four days later, on July 25, 1628, and this time the Pope himself presided. Three possible methods of dealing with Lucaris were discussed. The first was to establish proceedings against him before the Roman Inquisition. The second was to establish proceedings before a

Synod of Greek patriarchs and bishops. And the third was the usual way of bribery, both in connection with the Greek clerics who had the right of electing the Patriarch and in connection with the Turkish authorities. After much deliberation, the third of these methods was adopted as the most effective. The *Congregatio*, however, was not willing to proceed with the application of this method without first ascertaining that it was right and just according both to human and divine law, as if this were the first time that the Roman authorities had recourse to bribery in their efforts to get rid of Cyril. A questionnaire was therefore submitted to the Inquisition on the following points: Whether according to divine and human law it was permissible to use bribery in order to bring about Cyril's deposition; whether it was worthy of the dignity of the Holy See to have recourse to such a method; whether it was more worthy of the dignity of the Holy See to spend this money in bribing the Turks or in bribing the Greek bishops who had a part in the election of the Patriarch; whether this deposition could be rendered just and honest by any other means.[20]

It took the Holy Office a long time to complete its investigations before giving an answer to the above questionnaire. On August 19, 1628, the Pope charged Cardinals Millini and Scaglia to hasten the Lucaris case, whereupon the Inquisition immediately began its long sessions. At last on March 23, 1629, the Pope informed the *Congregatio* that the Holy Office approved of the deposition of Cyril and declared that it was quite in accordance with divine and human law to use bribery in order to bring about this desirable end.[21]

These decisions of the *Congregatio*, which would be executed by the Capuchins and Father Joseph behind the scenes and the imperial ambassador Rudolph Schmidt Schwarzenhorn in Constantinople, open up a new period in the struggle of the Church of Rome against Cyril and his reformation work. These decisions, however, took effect after 1628 ended; but we cannot leave this year yet, because in the course of it another event occurred, probably the most important in the whole of Cyril's adventurous career.

CHAPTER 11

CONFESSIO FIDEI

SITUATED IN ONE OF THE VALLEYS OF PIEDMONT, in the Italian Alps, was the Church of St. Martin's, whose pastor was a young man, the Rev. Antoine Leger. One day late in February 1628, a letter came to the elders of the Church of St. Martin's from the local Synod of the Reformed Church conveying to them a request of the Company of Pastors and Professors of the Church in Geneva to the effect that their pastor should be released from his charge in order to be sent to Constantinople to take up his duties as the chaplain of the Dutch Embassy. The Dutch ambassador in Constantinople had asked for a young theologian, well versed in Hebrew and Greek and able to preach in Italian, the most widely spoken European language at that time in the Levant, and who would be willing to be appointed chaplain to the Embassy, for, the ambassador went on to say, "there are at the present time great openings for the Gospel."[1] After much deliberation, the Company of Pastors and Professors decided to ask Leger to fill this place, as he was a man who "had the talents necessary for the requirements of such a calling."[2] Leger was not at all willing to accept this "call," because, as he put it in his answer, "he did not feel himself to be the suitable person for the duties of such a post" and because, moreover, he felt very uneasy about leaving his church.[3] Still less willing was the Church of St. Martin's to lose its pastor. So the *anciens* of the valleys in their reply of March 15 to the Company of Geneva expressed their regret that it was quite impossible for them to agree to the proposed transference of the Rev. Antoine Leger, in view of the excellent work which he was doing, not only in his own church but also throughout the valleys.[4]

A second meeting of the Company was held in Geneva and on March 24 another letter was dispatched to the "Pastors of the Valleys" signed by Prevost; Turretin, the famous Swiss divine; Diodati, the translator of the Bible into Italian; and Chabroy, in which they expressed their sympathy for the reluctance of the *anciens* of the valleys to release Leger but at the same time insisted on the absolute necessity of his release, in order that he might undertake work of far greater importance. Another letter, in the same spirit, was addressed to the people of St. Martin's Church, and still another one to Leger himself.[5] Further communications from the pastors of the valleys were received and a meeting of the Company was held in Geneva on the second of June 1628, at which Leger himself was present in order to state the reasons for which both he and his church were opposed to this separation. But the members of the Company were adamant in their insistence that he should proceed immediately to Constantinople. So Turretin, one of the members of the Company, was charged to write accordingly to the Dutch ambassador and to the Patriarch of Constantinople, who had expressed a personal interest in this matter.[6]

Shortly afterward Antoine Leger bade farewell to the valleys and to the people of his church, and early in the autumn of the same year he arrived in Constantinople[7] to take up his duties as chaplain to the Dutch ambasador and—what is of greater interest to us—to become Cyril's closest friend, to share with him the experiences of the remaining years of his adventurous career, and to assist him in the completion of the two greatest works of his life.

Cyril was at that time in sore need of a new friend, as only a few months earlier his old and trusted friend, Sir Thomas Roe, had left Constantinople[8] and Cyril had lost his powerful protector. And although Sir Peter Wych, the new English ambassador, did not refuse his assistance to Lucaris, he did not fashion the same ties of friendship as those which had linked Lucaris with Sir Thomas Roe. In the following ten years, therefore, the center of gravity in the matter of the diplomatic assistance given to Lucaris, moves from the English to the Dutch embassy in Constantinople. It was probably on the occasion of Sir Thomas Roe's departure and in his desire to express his feelings of gratitude for the kindness and protection he had received from the ambassador of England that Cyril sent as a gift to King Charles I of England the famous manuscript *Codex Alexandrinus*, which is today one of the treasures of the British Museum.

Leger's first impressions of the spiritual condition of the people in Constantinople were not at all favorable. In writing to the Company of Pastors and Professors of the Church in Geneva a few months after his arrival in Constantinople he says: "The ignorance of the people and of the majority of the clergy is something that is beyond belief . . . And what is worse, one can detect among the people very little desire, or none at all, to be instructed in spiritual things."[9] In the same letter he states that the two most important needs of the Greek people at the time were: "that the Holy Scriptures should be given to the people in a language which can be understood by them" and also "a small Catechism and other elementary helps necessary for the children." In both these undertakings, necessary for the reformation of the Greek Church, Leger was to give his invaluable assistance to the Patriarch. As early as March 1629, he was able to announce to the Company of Geneva, in connection with the preparation of an edition of the New Testament in Modern Greek, that "the work has happily begun and one wishes that it should make good progress." This was a big undertaking which required many years before it was completed. For this reason the first edition of the New Testament in Modern Greek did not appear until nine years later—a fitting crown of his life and work.

Burdened as he was with his various concerns, Cyril entrusted the translation of the New Testament to a good friend of his, the learned monk Maximus Callioupolites. He followed the progress of this work with great interest, however, and when the translator died while the book was still being printed, Lucaris read the proofs.[10] This first translation of the New Testament into Modern Greek was published in Geneva by P. Aubert. In this edition the two texts, the ancient and the translated, were printed in two parallel columns, with a few references and comments in the margin.

Even from a clearly literary point of view this translation is an extremely interesting work. It is another testimony to the courageous spirit of Lucaris, for it was very daring indeed to offer the sacred text of the Scriptures to the people in a language which was considered "vulgar," but which was the only one they were able to understand.

The Patriarch himself prefaces this first edition of the New Testament in Modern Greek. In his preface Cyril says that the gospel, written in the language which the people speak, is "a sweet message, given to us from heaven." That the duty of all Christians as regards this message is "to know and be acquainted with all its contents" and that there is no other way of learning about "the things that concern faith correctly . . . save through the divine and sacred Gospel." He sternly denounces those who forbid the people to study the Bible, as well as those who reject the translation of the original text: "If we speak or read without understanding, it is like throwing our words to the wind." Now that the Greek people have the New Testament in a language they can understand, they also have the duty to read it. And in concluding the preface, he says: "While you are all reading this divine and holy Gospel in your own tongue, appropriate the profit derived from its reading, and pray for those who have made this benefit possible for you, and may God ever lighten your way to that which is good. Amen."

The second project, however, the preparation of a Catechism through which to teach the elements of Christian faith to the people, was easier to attain, and so it made its appearance shortly after Leger arrived in Constantinople.

The preparation of such a Catechism was, as we have seen, one of Cyril's plans even before Leger's arrival, and no doubt it would have seen the light of day much earlier had not the Jesuits interfered with the printing operations of Metaxas. It seems, however, that the arrival of the enthusiastic young preacher from the Pedemondese valleys was largely responsible for the revival of this old plan, and a few months after Leger had settled in the Dutch Embassy he was able to dispatch the Patriarch's manuscript to Geneva, where the first Latin edition of what has since been known as the famous *Confessio Fidei* of Cyril was printed in March 1629. This first edition was dedicated to Cornelius van Haga, the Dutch ambassador, who had shown a deep and lasting interest in the work of the Patriarch. This Latin edition was soon followed in 1631 by another in Greek and Latin, and by a third edition in French which, however, bears no indication of the place where it was printed. Shortly afterward three more French translations appeared, two of which were printed in Sedan and the third in Amsterdam. Numerous translations in other European languages followed. An English edition was printed in London and another one was prepared by William Rait, under the title *A Vindication of the Reformed Religion, from the Reflections of a Romanist,* and was printed by John Forbes in Aberdeen in 1671. In his edition Rait had intended to give both the Greek text of the *Confessio* and his English translation, so that the reader might be able to judge for himself about the accuracy of the translation and "adversaries can neither justly load us with noveltie of tenets, or paucitie of adherents: and he who will peruse both Confessions, may easily convince them of their errour." Unfortunately, however, the printer discovered at the last minute that the amount of Greek type available would not permit him to set in print the entire Greek text, so Rait confined himself to having only the beginning of each article printed in Greek.

The *Confessio* consists of eighteen articles followed by four questions and their answers. At the end of each article and of each question a number of Scripture references serve to vindicate the truth of the *Confessio*. The first and fourth articles deal with the doctrine of the Godhead—the triune God—and the doctrine of the Creation. After dealing with the doctrine of the Godhead, Lucaris examines in the second article the Holy Scriptures as the source of divine revelation. And what he says or leaves unsaid in this chapter is very characteristic of his theological position. He keeps silent concerning the theory that sacred tradition as a source of revelation is equal in value to the Holy Scriptures. Even more characteristic is what he says concerning the superior authority of the Holy Scriptures in respect to the authority of the Church: "We believe . . . the testimony of the Holy Scriptures to be far superior to that of the Church. For it is not the same to be instructed by the Holy Spirit as by men. Man may sin or be deceived through ignorance. The Holy Scriptures neither deceive nor are deceived, nor are they liable to err, but are infallible and of everlasting authority."

In the third article Lucaris deals with the controversial problem of predestination and takes his stand as a follower of this doctrine. He examines it from its two aspects: the divine and the human. On the part of God the choice of man for salvation is an expression of divine sovereign will—"God's power and dominion." This expression of will, however, is not arbitrary because, with regard to man, it is dependent on the everlasting moral laws of justice, "the laws and rules of good order." And he concludes this article with the assurance that "God is merciful but just withal."

Related to the problem of predestination is that of Divine Providence in the governing of the universe, certain manifestations of which are beyond our comprehension. It is at this point that faith must assert itself and rest upon God's goodness and wisdom, as we are unable "to understand of our own the ways of Providence. Therefore in all humility we are of the opinion that we should rather be silent than indulge in superfluous talk which is not constructive."

In the sixth article the *Confessio* takes up the thread of the history of man from his creation to his grievous fall, the fruits of which he still continues to taste in his life. But the next article introduces the catharsis of this tragedy through the redeeming work of Jesus Christ. This work was accomplished through the kenosis which the Son of God underwent, an act by which in addition to His divine substance He assumed human flesh. And His purpose was to "grant salvation and glory to all believers" through His death and resurrection.

The present-day expression of this work of the Lord, as the eighth article puts it, is His presence at the right hand of the Father and His intercession for His own. He needs no assistance in this as He alone carries out the "work of the true and genuine High Priest and Mediator, and therefore He alone cares for His own." This again is very characteristic of the theological position of Lucaris.

In the ninth article Cyril touches upon the question about which Christians have been at variance with each other, namely, that of salvation by faith or salvation through works, and he declares himself unreservedly on the side of the former. For although he states his belief that "No one is saved without faith, the faith in Jesus Christ which justifies," he makes not the slightest allusion to works as a means of justification and the salvation of man.

This does not mean that Lucaris finds no place for works in the Christian life. In the thirteenth article he comes back to the question of man's justification and here he is even more emphatic. "We believe that man is justified by faith and not by works." It is only faith, he says, that can bring us into contact with Christ's justice and save us, while concerning works he declares that "they are not at all sufficient to make their author stand boldly before Christ's tribune and worthily claim his reward and be saved." He gives, however, special importance to works, not as a basis for the salvation of man but as a proof and fruit thereof, "in testimony to faith for the establishing of our calling."

The result of salvation by faith is regeneration, of which the *Confessio* speaks in the fourteenth article. It describes with very dark colors the state of the soul before regeneration, which is unable to save itself exactly like him "who went down from Jerusalem to Jericho and who could do or accomplish nothing by himself." Only the grace of God can save man from this hopeless state: "In order that one may do that which is good it is necessary that grace should go before."

In three of its articles, the tenth, eleventh, and twelfth, the *Confessio* takes up the subject of the Church. First, it makes a clear distinction between the invisible Church to which only those who have been chosen to eternal life belong, and the visible Church in which "wheat and chaff are mixed together." Cyril recognizes Christ as the Head of the Church and rejects the ascription of this title to any other human being. He accepts the Holy Spirit as the Teacher and Sanctifier of the "sojourning" Church, as he calls the visible Church militant here below. But he rejects the doctrine of the infallibility of the Church: "For it is true and certain that it is possible for the Church to err on its way, and to choose falsehood instead of truth. From this error and deceit, however, only the teaching and the light of the all holy Spirit can give release, and not that of any other human being."

In articles fifteen, sixteen, and seventeen, the *Confessio* deals with the sacraments, which, in line with his theological position, Lucaris accepts as two: "We believe the Gospel sacraments in the Church to be those which the Lord has delivered in the Gospels; and these are two. Because two have been delivered unto us. And the law-maker has delivered no more." What is especially noteworthy in this section of the *Confessio* is that Lucaris rejects the *ex opere operato;* that is, the reception of grace through the proper performance of the sacraments. In order that participation in those sacraments should have its effect in the heart of man, it should be "combined with genuine faith, because when the faith of the communicants is lessened, the completeness of the sacrament is not preserved."

These two sacraments are the Baptism and the Eucharist. With regard to Baptism, Cyril seems to deviate from the teaching of the Gospels, for he accepts that through Baptism the sins of the baptized are forgiven and regeneration is accomplished in his heart. "Wherefore, we do not doubt that, as ordered in the Gospel, the sins of those so baptized are forgiven, both the ancestral and those which the one baptized had committed. Thus those who are washed in the name of the Father and of the Son and of the Holy Spirit are regenerated, cleansed and justified."

Concerning the sacrament of the Eucharist, he accepts that it ensures for the communicant believer "the real and certain presence of our Lord Jesus Christ." He does not accept, however, this presence of the Lord in any material form, as in the doctrine of transubstantiation, which Cyril in his *Confessio* rejects emphatically. The believer truly partakes in this sacrament of the body of the Lord; not, however, with his teeth: "not through the chewing and dissolving of the communion by the teeth physically," but spiritually and by faith: "which in a spiritual way faith offers and gives freely to us." Cyril does not fail to repeat here that this presence of the Lord is secured "only if we believe; if we do not believe we are deprived of all profit from the sacrament."

The final article deals with the state of the dead, who are either in heavenly joy or in condemnation. "Those who have been justified in this present life, are not liable to condemnation; those who have not been justified before they slept, are ordained unto eternal condemnation. This makes it clear that we cannot give heed to the fable of the Purgatory, but we declare that each one must repent now and seek the forgiveness of his sins through the Lord Jesus Christ, if he wants to be saved."

The first of the four questions which are appended to the *Confessio* deals with the right of every Christian to read the Scriptures. The answer Cyril gives is that the reading of the Scriptures is the inalienable right of every Christian. The second question introduces the problem whether every Christian is able to understand the meaning of the Scriptures when he reads them. Cyril in his answer admits that there are many difficult passages in the Scriptures; the doctrines of the faith, however, are clear to those who have been born again and have been enlightened by the Holy Spirit. In reply to the third question, which deals with the canonical books of the Bible, Cyril says that the canonical books are those that have been recognized as such by the Council of Laodicea. And in answer to the final question about image worship, Cyril quotes the commandment: "Thou shalt not make unto thee a graven image, nor the likeness of any form that is in heaven above, or that is in earth beneath . . . Thou shalt not bow down thyself unto them, nor serve them." Cyril does not forbid the use of icons, but rejects, unreservedly, their worship and adoration, "so that we may not come to worship colors and art and created things, in place of the Maker and Creator."

With the wish, "May the Lord grant to all right-mindedness and a pure conscience," ends this Confession, which led its author to a martyr's death and which has not ceased to be, even after the death of its author, "a sign which shall be spoken against." With one sole exception it is imbued, as we have seen, with the gospel teaching, and stands unto this day a monument to the love of its author for the truth of the gospel and to the courage with which he preached it.

It is no wonder that a *Confessio Fidei* of such contents should rouse the antagonism of all those who did not favor the Reformation movement which Cyril had started within the Greek Church.

Cyril's first encounter over his *Confessio* was with the new ambassador of France, Count de Marcheville, who had succeeded De Cesy.

According to a letter of the Dutch ambassador, Van Haga, preserved in Smith's *Collectanea*,[11] on the twenty-second of December 1631 the Patriarch paid a visit of welcome to the new ambassador of France, who received him very courteously, addressing him as "Your Eminence," which was the title that had recently been accorded to cardinals. When the dinner, to which the ambassador had invited the Patriarch to stay, was over, the ambassador produced a copy of the *Confessio* and asked him whether he recognized it as his own and whether he persisted in adopting the doctrines proclaimed therein as his own. The Patriarch took the book in his hands and after one glance answered that it was his indeed; but he went on to say that before anyone questioned his right to adopt the doctrines contained therein, he should first be able to convince him through the Word of God that these doctrines contained errors. "I am under no obligation whatever," he added, "to give an account of my beliefs to the Pope. There are the metropolitans and the bishops of the Greek Church, and to these, assembled in a Council, I am ready to justify my position, by reference to the Word of God and to the early Fathers of the Church." To this the ambassador replied that in Rome and France "His Eminence" was considered to be a Calvinist, and that it would be much better for him if he were a Catholic, like the King himself, from whose favor and generosity he had much to gain. Cyril put an end to this conversation by saying, "In the matter of my beliefs and my eternal salvation, I shall obey neither the King of France nor any other person in the world, but shall strictly follow the dictates of my conscience."

This was, however, only the beginning. At the end of his Confession, Cyril himself had foretold that "this Confession of ours will be a sign which is spoken against." And such it has been indeed ever after. In Cyril's own lifetime at least three repudiations of the *Confessio* were circulated: one written by J. M. Caryophylles, the pro-Roman Archbishop of Iconium, in 1632; a second by the Dutch theologian Van Tillen; and a third one by the French François de la Bérandière, Bishop of Perigueux. It is characteristic that the book of J. M. Caryophylles was dedicated to Pope Urban VIII.

In September 1638, three months after Cyril's death, a Synod was held in Constantinople, presided over by his successor, another Cyril, the former Bishop of Berroea, which proceeded to anathematize both Cyril and his *Confessio*. In the document which embodies the decisions of this Synod the whole *Confessio*[12] is being submitted to the scrutiny of the body, point by point, and thirteen times it is reiterated that: "Cyril Lucaris who lays down in his Confession such beliefs be accursed." And at the bottom of these thirteen curses are the signatures of Cyril, the Patriarch of Constantinople; of Metrophanes Critopoulos, the Patriarch of Alexandria, former friend and protégé of Lucaris; of Theophanes, the Patriarch of Jerusalem; of twenty-four archbishops and bishops, as well as of twenty-one dignitaries of the Church of Constantinople. No greater condemnation could have been brought against the lifework of Cyril by the Church which he had loved so much.

Two years later, in 1640, another Council, convened by the Metropolitan of Kiev, Peter Moghila, was held in Jassy, the capital of Moldavia, and by a formal declaration condemned the *Confessio*.[13]

In May 1642, a second Council was held in Constantinople, presided over by the then Patriarch of Constantinople, Parthenius, again with the same purpose of condemning Cyril's *Confessio*. The verdict of this Synod,[14] which was entered in the official Codes of the Church, was that the entire *Confessio*, with the only exception of its seventh article, was stained by the "Calvinist heresy" and alienated from the faith of the Greek Church. "Hence the entire Holy Synod," says the formal document, "having examined carefully all these articles and investigated the meaning thereof, found all of them, with the exception of the seventh, adhering to Calvinistic heresy, and differing greatly from the religion of the Eastern Church." And after the minute examination and condemnation of the contents of the *Confessio* this historic document concludes as follows: "For this reason, we, the Holy Synod, unanimously reject completely these articles as well as the questions and banish them from our midst, as replete with

heresies and wholly alien to our orthodox religion, and we pronounce their author a stranger to our faith, proclaiming to all that
he lies against us when he claims that his own faith is the Eastern
Confession of the Christian faith of the Greeks."

About the same time a private condemnation of the *Confessio*
was circulated by a certain monk by the name of Arsenius, who
does not hesitate to call Cyril "a wicked and disorderly person,
who placed his own private interests above everything else."

Thirty years later, in 1672, another Council, convened by the
Patriarch of Jerusalem, Dositheus, was held in Jerusalem, or, to
be more correct, in Bethlehem. It is therefore known both as
Council of Jerusalem and Council of Bethlehem. This Council
also proceeded to anathematize the *Confessio*,[15] found the judgment of the Council of Constantinople just, and condemned Cyril
who "was made a Patriarch . . . through the assistance of the
Dutch Ambassador." It seems, however, that this Synod was
divided between two aims. The one was to prove that Cyril could
not have been the author of such a heretical confession, and for
this purpose it calls upon the testimony of some of his sermons
as contradicting ten of the articles of the *Confessio*. The other
trend was to condemn him if he was really a heretic, and so calls
him "the father of impiety" and "a wretch." The Patriarch of
Jerusalem, Dositheus, who presided over this Synod, writes:
"When Cyril Lucaris first became a Patriarch he was as Orthodox
as before and died in the communion of the Church . . . but that
he was a crypto-heretic is evident from many indications, although these were carried out secretly and stealthily."[16]

Thus this Synod marks the beginning of a persistent endeavor
on the part of many scholars, chiefly of the Greek Orthodox communion, to prove that the *Confessio* was not Cyril's own work.
And in this aspect also the *Confessio* has ever since been "a sign
which is spoken against," even as its author had foretold. A. Diomedes Kyriakos, in his church history, declares: "It is not known
who the author of this Confession was. It seems most probable
that it was the Jesuits who published it, so that they might in-
criminate their enemy Cyril."[17] M. Gedeon, on the other hand,
in his *Lists of Patriarchs*,[18] maintains that "a certain Confession
which was published in Geneva in 1628 must have certainly been

published by the Protestants, if not by some Papist, and circulated under the name of Lucaris." Chrysostom Papadopoulos, professor in the University of Athens, and later Archbishop of Athens, also attributes the authorship of the *Confessio* to a Protestant and expresses the belief that it was the personal work of Antoine Leger.[19] Along the same line Professor A. Diamantopoulos[20] writes: "Leger committed an immoral act, an act of blackmail against the representatives of the Greek Church, by which he intended to bind them in favor of Protestantism. He wrote himself a 'Confessio Fidei' and sent it to Geneva to be published, as though it had emanated from the Patriarchs of Constantinople, Alexandria and Jerusalem." An earlier writer, Sathas,[21] writes: "The Confessio Fidei which has been attributed to Lucaris was written by the Protestants." E. Velanidiotes[22] denies that this "spurious Confessio" is a work of Lucaris, without, however, expressing an opinion as to its author. The same position is taken by C. Paparighopoulos[23] and J. Messoloras.[24]

Other Greek Orthodox divines and historians, however, accept the genuineness of the *Confessio*. Andronicos Demetracopoulos[25] asks: "How then can we regard this Confession spurious, since not even Lucaris himself, who lived nine years after its publication, did so, even though he had been thus urged or requested?" Ch. Androutsos[26] says: "This Confession is Cyril's work . . . This is testified by . . . the silence of Cyril, who in no wise ever wanted to denounce the Confession publicly, although he was exhorted from every quarter to do so." D. S. Balanos[27] writes: "Research has led us to the conclusion that Patriarch Cyril Lucaris is the author of the Confession attributed to him, and that he was prompted to write it by religious rather than political motives." Cyril's authorship of the *Confessio* is also admitted by M. Renieris,[28] B. Georgiades,[29] E. Zolotas,[30] and Professor J. Carmiris,[31] who, however, suggests that the Confession was the product of psychological pressure exerted on Cyril by his Calvinistic friends.

One can sympathize with the divines of the Greek Orthodox Church who find it so difficult to accept the fact that one of the greatest men who ever sat on the Ecumenical Throne of Constantinople was a Calvinist. But personal feelings should never be the criterion by which questions such as the above are settled. Rather should facts be considered dispassionately. And the facts which bear on the above issue all point to the Lucarian authorship of the *Confessio*.

There is first of all the fact that, although the *Confessio* appeared nine whole years before the Patriarch's martyrdom, the latter did not write a single line, not even the faintest hint, to deny that he had written it himself. Would not this silence have been altogether inexplicable had there been any truth to what has so often been suggested, although with no positive proof; that is, that the hand of a Calvinist of the West had written the *Confessio* and had attributed it to the Patriarch of Constantinople in order to give it validity? Inexplicable, because the publication of the *Confessio* was undoubtedly the great event of the day, and the Roman Catholic enemies of Cyril used it as a weapon in their struggle to get rid of him, representing him to the people of his Church as one who had betrayed his faith by declaring openly that he was a Calvinist. This must have damaged considerably his position in the circles of his Church, and Cyril would not have tolerated the damage caused to him by the publication of this Calvinistic *Confessio* over his name, especially at such a troublous time. If we were to suppose that Cyril was not the author of the *Confessio*, the simplest thing for him to do would have been to deny the authorship of the book and thus be saved from the new difficulty which had so suddenly been added to all his other problems. But Lucaris did nothing of the kind.

We referred to Cyril's silence in the matter of the authorship of the *Confessio* as one of the most common arguments for its genuineness. The silence was not, however, absolute. Three years after the publication of the *Confessio*, Diodati of Geneva sent Lucaris a copy of his Italian translation of the Bible and in a letter written on April 15, 1632,[32] to acknowledge the receipt of this gift, the Patriarch referred to his own *Confessio*. It appears that Diodati had asked him whether he had published anything of his own and Cyril answered: "At present I have published nothing but the Confession of Faith." Doubts about the genuineness of the *Confessio* apparently had been raised even at that time, for he adds: "Here in Constantinople many copies of my

Confession have been made and a number of my friends have requested me to authenticate some with my own hand, which I did not refuse them. But now they no longer need copies published with my signature, for the reasons which I will presently make known to you"—and he proceeds to give an account of his meeting with the French ambassador and the public declaration which he had made that the *Confessio* was his own work. This, he thought, ought to put an end to all doubts on this point. The same unequivocal statement concerning the authorship of his *Confessio* he made in a letter to Leger on the sixteenth of July 1635,[33] in which he writes that his *Confessio* had dealt a heavy blow at the heart of the Papists. Likewise, in another undated letter to the same person,[34] he expounds and supports the contents of some of its articles.

In support of the genuineness of the *Confessio* we have, further, the numerous letters which Cyril sent to the Protestant divines Uytenbogaert, Le Leu de Wilhem, Leger, and others. The genuineness of the letters was never, so far as we know, questioned by those who reject the Lucarian authorship of the *Confessio*. In these letters, however, the doctrines of the *Confessio* are expounded in a fuller and more systematic way.

Thus—to mention a few only of the controversial points of his theological position—in his letter to De Dominis of September 6, 1618,[35] he proclaims that the invocation of the saints overshadows the glory of the Lord. This is exactly what is stressed in the eighth article of his *Confessio*. In the fourteenth article of the *Confessio* he writes that free will is dead in a man who has not been regenerated, because it is only through the help of divine grace that free will can act. This same principle is expressed in his letter of September 6, 1618, to De Dominis,[36] in which he says that free will "is dead in the unregenerate." In articles fifteen to seventeen of his *Confessio*, speaking of the sacraments, he accepts only two: Baptism and the Holy Eucharist. And in his letter to De Dominis written on September 22, 1613,[37] he again accepts only two sacraments. In regard particularly to the Holy Eucharist, he denies, in the seventeenth article of his *Confessio*, the doctrine of transubstantiation, as he had done previously in a number of letters. In writing to De Dominis he calls transubstantiation a "chimaera." In a letter to Leger on April 14, 1635,[38] he rejects with fine irony the doctrine which "out of a piece of bread or a crumb creates a Jesus Christ." In writing to the same on March 10, 1636,[39] he says that "the word transubstantiation is well pleasing to the uneducated." In answer to the fourth question, at the end of his *Confessio,* he rejects the worship of images. And in a letter to De Dominis written on September 6, 1618,[40] he expresses in striking language his sorrow at the sight of image worship in the East, a worship which "is due to God alone." Therefore the genuineness of the *Confessio* cannot very well be rejected, unless these letters also are proved to be forgeries.

Finally, in support of the Cyrillian authorship of the *Confessio* we have the testimony of the Synods of the Greek Church. As has already been stated, in four different Synods that were held after Cyril's death, the *Confessio* was officially condemned. Of these condemnations the most important for us is the one by the Synod of Constantinople in 1638. And this because the above Synod was closer to the events and made its decisions before the expediency for ridding the memory of the great Patriarch from the stigma of Calvinism began to exert its influence within the official circles of the Orthodox Church. Among the leaders of the Church who took part in that Synod and condemned the *Confessio* and anathematized its author, was the Patriarch of Alexandria, Metrophanes Critopoulos. We know what a debt of gratitude Critopoulos owed to Cyril, with whom he was united by ties of mutual respect and affection up to his death. And one can imagine the bitterness of the task with which Critopoulos was confronted when he was called upon to sign the document in which the memory of his friend and benefactor was cursed. It is certain that had there been a way of escape open for him, Critopoulos would have taken it. Had there been the slightest doubt in his mind that Cyril was indeed the author of the *Confessio,* Critopoulos would certainly have refused to affix his signature to that document. If, then, the Act of the Synod of Constantinople bears the signature of the Patriarch of Alexandria, this can only mean that in the mind of Cyril's contemporaries, friends as well as foes, there was not the shadow of a doubt that the *Confessio* was his own work.

In still another sense the *Confessio* became a sign spoken against. Some of the scholars who accept the book as a genuine work of Lucaris, maintain that it does not express Cyril's real feelings and convictions. And they attribute to him very mean motives in writing it. The first to accuse Lucaris of such motives was the well-known Hugo Grotius, who in his *Votum pro pace ecclesiastica*[41] says that "Cyril of Constantinople was moved by considerations political, not theological, when he wrote his 'Confessio.'" The same line was followed by A. Arnauld,[42] who says that "when Cyril wrote to de Wilhem in 1619 . . . he did it against his own conscience." And further: "The Calvinists of Geneva and Holland could not have approved of that criminal dissimulation." It is not easy, however, to estimate Arnauld's exact opinion concerning Lucaris and his theological position, as in the same book[43] he goes on to say that it was an act of hypocrisy on Cyril's part when he accepted his appointment to the Ecumenical Throne, as "he should have regarded that office to be incompatible with the doctrines of the religion which he secretly professed to be the only true one."

G. J. Arvanitides, one of the modern writers, also attributes the writing of the *Confessio* to political motives.[44] A. Diamantopoulos,[45] while rejecting the genuineness of the *Confessio*, suggests that Cyril, being in need of powerful friends in his struggle against the Church of Rome, would probably be willing to sacrifice some of his religious principles in order to secure the help of the Protestant powers. To anyone, however, who has even the remotest acquaintance with Lucaris and his work, it is evident that this is an unwarrantable judgment. For, why should Lucaris make concessions in the matter of principles in order to secure the protection of the Protestant powers when these were, for reasons of their own, only too anxious to grant him that protection and make him their ally against the French ambitions in the Near East? Lucaris was undoubtedly a clever man, and it could not have taken him long to realize that his own interests coincided with those of England and Holland in the Near East; and that he could be sure of the support of these two powers without going so far as to publish a Calvinistic Confession of Faith which he did not believe.

There remains a last point to be considered in connection with the *Confessio*. Granted that Lucaris was the author of the book and that he wrote it not from questionable motives but in order to give expression to his religious convictions, still the question is raised: Was Cyril entitled to attribute these convictions to the Greek Church as a whole and to present his *Confessio* not as an exposition of his own individual beliefs but as an outline of the faith of the Greek Church itself?

In answering this question we should bear in mind that so far as the Greek Church was concerned, its doctrine had never been defined in the sense in which the Council of Trent had defined the doctrine of the Church of Rome. The Council of Trent had crystallized in a clear and definite way the dogma of the Roman Church, while the doctrine of the Greek Church had been allowed to remain in a fluid condition. According to the Greek Church, only an Ecumenical Council has the authority to define the doctrine of the Church, and since an Ecumenical Council had not met for many centuries, the official doctrine of the Greek Church had been left in a state far less definite than the minutely defined dogma of the Church of Rome. In the course of time a number of practices which were more in accordance with the Roman tradition than with the simplicity of the Evangelical belief had crept into the ritual of the Greek Church. These practices, however, were and still are lacking the sanction of an Ecumenical Council, and, strictly speaking, they cannot be considered to be part of the doctrine of the Greek Church. At the time of which we are speaking there seems to have been the practice for everyone who published a Confession of his faith to ascribe that Confession to the whole of the Greek Church. This practice was followed by Critopoulos,[46] Dositheus of Jerusalem,[47] and Moghilla.[48] But, to quote Professor Hamilcar Alivisatos, of the Faculty of Divinity in the University of Athens: "The so-called Orthodox Confessions, which are usually cited both by Orthodox and non-orthodox writers as official statements of orthodox doctrine, are no longer recognized as such by most modern theologians, because ... these confessions have not the authority of an Ecumenical Synod."[49] And Professor J. Carmiris, of the chair of symbolics in the same university,[50] in dealing with the Confession which

Metrophanes Critopoulos published, exonerates the writer from the blame of having misrepresented the doctrine of the Greek Church, because, as he says, "the Greek Church had not as yet declared itself officially concerning the questions which had been raised mainly by the Reformation, nor had the Greek theologians investigated and defined exactly the points of contact or disagreement between the Greek Church and the Protestant Churches." Renieris[51] deals with this question even more clearly when he says: "During Cyril's lifetime the Greek Church had not yet expressed definite opinions on the new points which the Reformation had raised in the West, and consequently . . . it was possible for Cyril to believe that the calvinistic interpretation of the texts was in accord with the spirit of his Church, and that if different interpretations and contrary practices prevailed among the Greeks, this was due to the superstition which resulted from the decline and subjugation of the nation." Or as D. S. Balanos puts it: "He probably thought, in his delusion, that by his assumption of calvinistic principles, the orthodox principles were not shaken but were only cleansed and clarified in accordance with the Gospel and that they were completed and freed from human additions."[52]

Such being the case, it follows that although Cyril Lucaris' *Confessio* was undoubtedly in most of its articles not in agreement with the popular religious feeling of his time, which had been very deeply influenced by the teaching of the Roman Church, it could nevertheless claim that it stood much nearer the official standards of the Greek Church, as these had been set down by the Ecumenical Councils, than the writings of his Romanizing adversaries. It will be remembered that Cyril himself, in his answer to the challenge of the French ambassador, had stated that he was prepared to examine the contents of his *Confessio* only in the light of the Scriptures and of the early Fathers of the Church. If these are the authorities of the doctrine of the Greek Church, Lucaris was not far wrong when he claimed that his *Confessio* was the expression of the doctrine of the Greek Church.

CHAPTER 12

NEW STORMS

HAD POPE URBAN VIII and the *Propaganda* the slightest desire to relax their warfare against Cyril, in the hope that by the use of more diplomatic means they might be able to win him over to their side, as they had done with so many other Greek clerics in the past, all such hope must have been dispelled by the appearance of Cyril's *Confessio*. If there were the shadow of a doubt in the mind of the Pope and his advisers about where Cyril actually stood, that doubt was now removed. Furthermore, it was now clear that the open declaration of his faith which Cyril had made, through the publication of his *Confessio,* precluded any change of his attitude toward the Roman Church, even if such a change were desirable. Therefore the duty of the Pope and the *Propaganda* was clear. As the Roman Catholic historian Von Pastor puts it, Cyril "constituted so imminent a peril for the Union that it was a duty for the Holy See to do its utmost to get him removed from the Patriarchal See."[1] New decisions were, therefore, taken against the hated Patriarch. The execution of the decisions, however, would be entrusted from now on not to the familiar hands of the French ambassador, but to those of the ambassador of the Emperor. It is true that the French ambassador does not disappear completely from our narrative; he is to play an occasional small part in giving effect to Rome's designs against Lucaris. The center of interest, however, has decidedly moved from the French Embassy to that of the Emperor.

This change of scenery in Constantinople was not due merely to the fact that De Cesy had suffered such a momentous defeat in the matter of Metaxas and the Jesuits. That must have helped, no doubt, to persuade the *Propaganda* that "notwithstanding all his zeal, De Cesy could not overthrow Lucaris singlehanded."[2] Other factors operating nearer Rome must have contributed to effect this change. For a long time an open feud had existed between two faithful daughters of Rome—France and Austria. This feud had created for Rome such a delicate state of affairs that it required great tact on the part of the Curia in handling these affairs, so that one Roman Catholic power should be balanced against the other to the benefit of Rome. Other popes before Urban VIII had to face the same problem. Thus, when Clement VIII was asked to give absolution to Henry IV, he was confronted with the problem of befriending the King of France without giving offense to the Spaniards.[3] And in dealing with a similar difficult situation Pope Leo X is reported to have said that "when a man has formed a compact with one party, he must none the less take care to negotiate with the other."[4] At the time, however, of the accession of Urban VIII things had reached a climax,[5] and at a moment when the balance slightly favored Austria, the *Propaganda* decided to take the initiative in the matter of Lucaris out of the hands of the French ambassador and commit it to those of the ambassador of Austria.

This coincided with the arrival of a new Austrian ambassador in Constantinople. The old ambassador, Baron von Kuefstein, was a Protestant and did not become a Roman Catholic until 1629. Rudolph Schmidt Schwarzenhorn, who succeeded him in 1629,[6] was a Roman Catholic and was eager to lend his assistance to the promotion of Rome's plans against the Patriarch, all the more so as this was in accord with the campaign which the Austrian Embassy had just launched to appropriate for the Emperor the right of protecting the Christian populations in Turkey, which so far had been a privilege of France. In order to forestall his Austrian colleague the French ambassador ordered that prayers be regularly offered for the King of France in all Roman Catholic churches in Constantinople. Schwarzenhorn imitated him at once, and this led to protests on the part of the French ambassador and to the creation of a confused and unpleasant state of affairs for the Roman Catholics in the Turkish capital.[7] Such was the atmosphere in which the fate of Lucaris and his movement of reformation was to be decided.

Shortly after Cyril's encounter with the French ambassador over the matter of his *Confessio,* which we mentioned in the previous chapter, two Greek bishops arrived in Constantinople.[8] They were the Metropolitans of Sophia and of Achrid, who, according to Van Haga, had been obliged to forsake their own country, on account of the evil life they had led, and take refuge in Rome. There, according to the same authority, the Pope and the *Propaganda* lost no time in enlisting them in their warfare against the Patriarch of Constantinople. When they arrived in that city they were given hospitality at the French Embassy and immediately started their operations. They began by spreading the rumor that Cyril was a "heretic," a "Lutheran," and an "infidel." Shortly afterward they made it known to the Greek bishops who had the right of electing the Patriarch that Rome intended to buy the Patriarchate from the Turkish authorities by paying an annual sum of money, and to appoint as Patriarch a man who would be willing to pay homage to the Roman See.

Whether there was any truth in the story that Rome intended to "purchase" the Patriarchate, it is difficult to say. Still more difficult is it to guess whether the Turks would be willing to sell at a fixed sum of money an office which had proved so profitable to them. It is, however, just another indication of the disrepute into which the office of the Patriarch had fallen through the petty-mindedness and the rivalries of the Greeks themselves. Cyril could not ignore such a serious threat and was obliged to take measures to avert this danger.

Unfortunately his great friend, Sir Thomas Roe, was no longer in Constantinople, and one can imagine how Cyril missed his wise counsel and strong protection in those anxious days. Sir Peter Wych, the successor of Sir Thomas Roe in the Embassy, was very friendly toward Cyril. In fact, De Cesy in a letter to De Chavigny[9] mentions that in 1635 the Patriarch baptized a son of the ambassador, to whom he gave his own name, Cyril. Now, however, under the influence of Archbishop Laud, English policy was much less inclined to associate itself with Calvinistic projects on the Continent,[10] and in spite of the friendliness shown to him by the English ambassador, Cyril soon discovered that he could no longer expect any real support from him.

The only person left to him was Van Haga, the Dutch ambassador, and to the very end Cyril enjoyed this man's friendship and support. Speaking of Van Haga, Cyril says: "The illustrious Cornelius van Haga . . . having towards me a pure friendship . . . did not miss any opportunity to show his love to us in all our calamities."[11] It does not appear, however, that on this occasion Van Haga's services were sought. Cyril confined himself to communicating with the bishops and other influential people of his own Church, to whom he disclosed the new danger which was now threatening them, and the decision was taken to make known to the Grand Vizir this new machination of the agents of Rome. This was done, and by the intervention of the Grand Vizir the danger was averted. Our sources do not tell us whether the payment of a certain sum of money was also required for the securing of the favor of the Grand Vizir. But it would be very surprising if this were not the case.

Cyril, however, was not allowed to enjoy peace for long. Another enemy made his appearance in the person of Cyril Contari, Bishop of Berroea. This was not the well-known Berroea of Macedonia, but a town of Syria, the present-day Aleppo. Cyril Contari was a disciple of the Jesuits,[12] and a graduate of their school in Constantinople.[13] By his blind obedience to Rome he had succeeded in infuriating almost every section of the Greek Church.[14] Contari was to become later Schwarzenhorn's favorite candidate for the Ecumenical Throne, and it is interesting to see just what Schwarzenhorn thought of his protégé: "He is a good and virtuous prelate: too good towards the evil ones and too severe towards the virtuous. Generous, when it is not necessary for him to be, and stingy when he should have been showing some liberality."[15] The unholy alliance of these two men, the ambassador of the Emperor of Austria and the Bishop of Berroea, was to bring about finally the death of Cyril and the end of his work. It is not quite certain, however, whether at this present stage Contari made any use of the assistance of Schwarzenhorn.

Contari's enmity for Lucaris dates back to the time when he had been appointed by the Patriarch locum tenens of the vacant

See of Thessalonica. When that See was to be permanently filled, Contari applied for it, but Lucaris refused this request as he had destined the See for Athanasius Patelarus, about whom more will be said presently. Contari was deeply hurt by the refusal of his request and decided to avenge himself. When, therefore, Cyril sent him to Russia and other countries in order to collect funds for the Church of Constantinople, he embezzled the money he had collected and proceeded to make use of it in October 1633 for the procuring of the Patriarchal Throne for himself.

It seems that at the suggestion of a certain Archimandrite Euthymius, slander was again used as a weapon before the Turks. Cyril was again falsely accused of being responsible for the continued incursions of the Cossacks.[16] The accusation came at a most opportune moment for the furtherance of the plans of Rome, for Constantinople had then been passing through a very troubled time. Following a big fire which had destroyed a considerable section of the capital, the people variously expressed hostile feelings toward the government, which in its turn reacted against this uprising of the people by a long series of cruel measures. The Sultan himself regularly made the rounds of the city by night, in order to seek out the revolutionary centers of the people, and as Von Hammer says in his history: "Every morning the bodies of the victims, left lying in the streets, testified to the relentless justice of the preceding night."[17]

In the midst of an atmosphere charged with anxiety and fear it was not in the least difficult for Cyril's enemies to make him suspicious to the Turks. And they succeeded actually in dethroning him in order to put Contari in his place—not for long, however, because Contari failed to raise the full sum of money promised to the Turks. And so, after enjoying the title of Ecumenical Patriarch for seven days, he was deposed and exiled to the island of Tenedos.[18]

Cyril, therefore, came back to his own, but only for a short time. In March 1634, he received another attack, once again from a fellow countryman, from whom he had reasons to expect gratitude. This was Athanasius Patelarus, for whose sake Cyril provoked the anger of Contari. Patelarus was a Cretan, quite famous for his erudition[19] and a great supporter of the Romanizing party within the Greek Church.[20] Having been elevated to the office of Archbishop of Thessalonica by Cyril himself, he forgot, in the course of time, his debt of gratitude to this man and in his turn aspired to the Ecumenical Throne. He offered to buy this office from the Turkish authorities and when they seemed unwilling to reduce even by one cent, as Smith very graphically puts it,[21] the price at which they had offered to sell the Throne to Contari, Patelarus paid the whole sum of money and entered into the Patriarchal office.

So Lucaris was sent to exile in the island of Tenedos. This was the third time that Cyril was ejected from his See and the second time he was sent into exile.[22] He did not stay very long in Tenedos, but long enough to exchange at least one letter with his new friend Antoine Leger of the Dutch Embassy. Writing to him on March 18, 1634,[23] from the island of his exile, Cyril thanks his friend for his letter—"It gave me a great consolation in my exile"—as well as for a few books which Leger had sent him.

The Dutch Embassy, however, did not confine itself to sending books and letters of consolation to the exiled Patriarch. They took measures to have him brought back to his See, and in three months' time, in June 1634, "with the great help of his friends and the payment of a large sum of money, Cyril came back to his own."[24]

Fleeing from the just indignation of the people, Patelarus went to Italy, where he asked for the protection and assistance of the Roman Church. He expressed, moreover, the wish to visit Rome and pay his respects to Pope Urban VIII, possibly with the secret hope that thus he would give the Pontiff the chance of offering him—as a reward for his iniquitous services—the cardinal's red hat.[25] Rome, however, who had proved during that troubled time that she knew how to benefit from treason without being under obligation to the traitor, not only refrained from giving him the cardinal's hat but did not even encourage his intended visit. She only confined herself to sending him a sum of money for his return trip to his native land.[26]

THE TWO CYRILS

W HAT REMAINS OF LUCARIS' STORY could well be described as the struggle between the two Cyrils—Cyril Lucaris and Cyril Contari.

Cyril returned from his second exile and was reinstated on the Patriarchal Throne in the month of June 1634. He was not permitted, however, to occupy the See for long, as new troubles broke out early in 1635. The exact date when these occurred is not given by our authorities. Smith confines himself to giving the year only.[1] Le Quien, on the other hand, says that the troubles occurred one year after the return of Lucaris to Constantinople— "*anno elapso*";[2] in this, however, he is not altogether accurate, as we possess letters written by Lucaris in Chios and Rhodes during his third exile, dated early in April 1635. It may be safe to agree with Hofmann[3] in placing the troubles in March 1635.

As soon as Contari found himself back in Constantinople, he promptly forgot the hardships of his exile in Tenedos. Incited by the representatives of Rome,[4] he resumed his efforts to secure for himself the Throne of Constantinople.

As things had turned out, this was not difficult to secure, provided the money could be found wherewith to pay the *peshkesh* to the Turkish authorities. This Contari managed to find. It is not known whence, as our authorities are silent on the matter, but it is most probable that he did so through the help of his Roman friends. At any rate, fifty thousand dollars was paid to the Turkish authorities and Cyril Contari found himself, once again, Ecumenical Patriarch "by the grace of the Turkish Emperor and the Roman Pontiff," according to the caustic phrase used by Smith in his *Collectanea—"Imperatoris Turcarum et*

Romanis Pontificis gratia."[5] And Cyril Lucaris found himself for the third time on the road to exile.

That some attempt had been made against Lucaris' life before he was eventually sent into exile is evident from the fact that as soon as he reached the island of Chios, the first stage of his journey, he wrote to Leger and gave thanks for "having been delivered out of the hands of his enemies."[6] Schwarzenhorn himself, in one of his reports to the Emperor Ferdinand III on the affair Lucaris, says that the Patriarch was at that time imprisoned for six days in a secret place and at the absolute disposal of Contari.[7] One of the bishops suggested, in the presence of the Austrian ambassador, that they should kill Lucaris, or that they should at least blind him and thus incapacitate him permanently for the office of the Patriarch. This suggestion was approved, Schwarzenhorn says, neither by himself nor by Contari. The reason for which the Austrian ambassador withheld his approval, as he himself discloses it in his report to the Emperor, was that very near the place where Cyril was kept as a prisoner dwelt a number of influential Greeks who would be certain to hear the cries of Lucaris, "and God only knows in what an unpleasant situation I might have found myself."

Schwarzenhorn, however, made another suggestion: Contari, or, as Schwarzenhorn calls him for convenience, the "Patriarch of Berroea," should spend some money in order to charter a ship manned by sailors of his absolute confidence who, under pretext of taking Lucaris to Rhodes or Cyprus, would lead him to Rome. The Porte would be easily persuaded to issue the passport and other necessary permits, in order to have the Patriarch sent to one of the islands in the Archipelago, as on previous occasions. Then arrangements would have to be made with some trustworthy Turk, who would see to it that the ship, instead of proceeding to Rhodes or Cyprus, would head for Malta or for the first ship of "Christian Pirates," which they might come across in the open sea. And so that neither the Turks nor the crew of the ship should run any risk of being hurt by the pirates, the Austrian ambassador would furnish them with the necessary permits and letters of recommendation. Soon after the ship's departure from Constantinople, the rumor would be ingeniously spread that the ship had an encounter with Maltese pirates, who had led Lucaris away to their island.

Contari gave his approval to this plan and left the care of finding a suitable ship and a trustworthy crew to the Austrian ambassador. Schwarzenhorn was not slow in concluding the business and soon a bargain was closed: eight hundred dollars for the ship and five hundred for the crew, the first of these sums to be paid in advance, the second to be paid as soon as the ship came back. Contari, however, found the sum required of him too large, and shortly after he informed Schwarzenhorn that he had arranged for the transportation of Lucaris to Rome on much cheaper terms and asked for the permits and the letters of recommendation to the "Christian Pirates." Schwarzenhorn sent the letters, "not, however, without some fear that some mismanagement might give the whole affair a bad turn." And what Schwarzenhorn was afraid of did eventually happen.

While Contari was searching for a cheaper ship, the Dutch ambassador was informed of the plan through his spies, "who," Schwarzenhorn complains, "are to be found everywhere." He managed to bribe the crew of the ship Contari had chartered and to secure their promise that as soon as they were out in the open sea, the bishop who was to accompany Cyril on his journey to the "Christian Pirates" would find himself "a prisoner of his prisoner." On the fixed day Cyril embarked on the ship, which immediately put out to sea. With a favorable wind it soon arrived at Chios where Cyril was given a warm welcome by the Governor of Rhodes, who had been spending a few days there. The latter was a friend of the Dutch ambassador and had been informed of Schwarzenhorn's plan and Van Haga's counterplan. He therefore took Cyril along with him to Rhodes and sent the escorting bishop back to Constantinople in great shame.

We have not only the records of Ambassador Schwarzenhorn and the historian Smith,[8] but Cyril himself gives an account in a letter to Leger[9] of this plan of his enemies to abduct and take him a prisoner to Rome, of its unforeseen collapse and the disgrace of those who had devised it.

Cyril was left in exile, in Rhodes, up to the month of July of the following year, 1636. That was a trying time for him. The persecutions and the hardships he had suffered began to tell on his spirit.

"I am in a garden," he writes to his friend Leger,[10] "and I taste of the fruits thereof, and they are all full of bitterness and pain." A vague foreboding of what the near future had in store for him had already crept into his mind: "These men know well that they cannot have success in their plans, so long as I am alive. . . . Your prayers will be a great help to me. . . . Nothing will befall me, which God will not permit."[11] And in another letter: "I lift my eyes to heaven, from whence cometh my help, as to all those who put their trust on the Almighty."[12]

While in that garden with the bitter fruits, however, he did not lose sight of the matters which were uppermost in his heart. He writes to Leger: "I have nothing to sustain me, but the contemplation of spiritual things."[13] Then he goes on to tell him how distressed he had been during a conversation with a fellow countryman of his in Chios, when the latter expressed the view that "Jesus Christ is only one of the Mediators, but there are others beside Him, less important, who also intercede for us." In the same letter he expresses himself very strongly against the doctrine of transubstantiation, which "out of a piece of bread creates a Jesus Christ."

At this trying time Leger's friendship meant much for Cyril, and the letters which he received from his Swiss friend were, as he himself admits, a source of consolation. Shortly after his arrival in Rhodes he received the manuscript of a book written by his friend on the subject of the Lord's Supper, and so great was his delight when he read it that he asked the author's permission to have it translated into modern Greek and circulated among his own people.[14] A few months later Nathaniel Conopius, a friend and follower of Lucaris, wrote to Leger that in a short while he was going to translate Leger's treatise "against the Papist Transubstantiation."[15] Very likely this is the same book about which Cyril had written from his exile and which he had now asked his friend Conopius to translate.

Back in Constantinople, finding himself an Ecumenical Patriarch, Cyril Contari gave himself unrestrainedly over to the enjoyment of his triumph. Banquets were organized for him and his friends, in which it seems that Contari did not set a very high example of sobriety. He also adopted a highhanded policy toward the clergy under him and persecuted the friends of Lucaris, some of whom he succeeded in having imprisoned. By these methods it was not long before he alienated himself from the influential people of the Church. This is testified not only by Smith,[16] whose friendly attitude toward Lucaris is well-known, but also by Contari's supporter, Schwarzenhorn, who, in his report to the Emperor,[17] gives an account of the foolish way in which Contari behaved while he occupied the Ecumenical Throne. What finally infuriated a large part of the clergy against him was the convocation on his part of a Synod in March 1636 in which he pronounced Lucaris deposed and anathematized. Three copies of the decision of this Synod were dispatched to Rome, one by the Roman Patriarchal Vicar in Constantinople, another by the ambassador, Schwarzenhorn, and a third one by a Jesuit of Chios.[18]

At long last a revolt against Contari broke out among the bishops in Constantinople. Confusion prevailed for a few weeks, but eventually the rebel bishops won and in a Synod which they convened they condemned Contari.[19] Thus was Contari deposed, after having occupied the See for sixteen months, and was sent into exile by the same ship by which Lucaris was to return to Constantinople. On the second of July, 1636, Leger wrote to the Society of the Pastors in Geneva: "We are now waiting for the return of the Confessor from his exile in Rhodes by the same ship, which will carry there the pseudo-patriarch."[20]

Cyril indeed returned to Constantinople, but for some unknown reason, probably connected with the famous *peshkesh*, he was not permitted to occupy the Throne at once. Thus on January 12, 1637, six whole months after Cyril's return to Constantinople, Nathaniel Conopius wrote to Leger in Geneva: "One of these days his Reverence will return to the Throne."[21] In the meantime the See was occupied by Neophytus, Archbishop of Heracleia.

It is not often, in the course of Lucaris' story, that one comes across a noble personality. It is therefore with a sense of relief that we take note of the appearance of Neophytus in this narrative of meanness, intrigue, and hatred. Neophytus was a disciple of Lucaris.[22] He shared Cyril's evangelical views, as is made clear by Leger's letter to the Pastors in Geneva of July 2, 1636: "He is more recommended by the integrity of his character than by his

erudition; nevertheless he has such a high opinion of the 'Confession' of his master, that in Crete, their common native-land,
the enemies of the truth are branding him with the same
heresies."[23] Neophytus had a deep respect and affection for his
teacher, and is one of the very few who did not repay Cyril's
kindness by ingratitude. While Cyril was in Rhodes, Neophytus
took a prominent part in the efforts which were made to secure
the return of the exiled Patriarch. And when the Patriarch at last
came, only to find that he would not be permitted to occupy his
See for some time, Neophytus occupied it, after making it clear
that this was a provisional arrangement and that he would retire
as soon as the lawful Patriarch would be permitted to exercise
his duties. Le Quien, following Cygala, states that Neophytus
acted as Patriarch for one year.[24] Strictly speaking, however,
Neophytus only acted as locum tenens for Lucaris, and when in
April 1637 the way was cleared for his master to return to the
Throne, he promptly retired.[25] The exact date of Cyril's last elevation to the Patriarchal Throne is not absolutely certain. Le
Quien says that Cyril exercised his Patriarchal duties for the last
time for a period of a year and five months. It is known that
Cyril's martyrdom was in June 1638. Le Quien's information,
therefore, places the beginning of Cyril's last Patriarchate in
January or February 1637.[26] This does not conflict with the above
information of Conopius.

The last chapter of Cyril's career was now about to open, and
the good Patriarch would have to face the adventures of this
period with fewer friends around him than ever before. For no
sooner had he come back to Constantinople than Leger left it
to return to his own country. Thus Cyril lost still another friend
at a time when he needed him most. In a letter which he addressed to the Society of the Pastors in Geneva on August 17,
1636, Cyril gave thanks for the work which Leger had done in
their midst. He admits that he is now about to face many more
troubles, but "the Lord is my Light and my Salvation, of whom
shall I be afraid?"[27]

Shortly afterward Leger's successor, Sartoris, arrived from
Geneva, and on December 2, 1636, the new chaplain to the Dutch
ambassador wrote to the Society of the Pastors in Geneva in

order to express his appreciation of "the gracious welcome which was accorded to me by the Patriarch."[28] The joy and encouragement, however, which the arrival of the new chaplain must have brought to Cyril did not last long, for a few months later on the eighth of September, 1637, A. Rivet wrote to Geneva to announce the death of the new chaplain.[29]

▣ CHAPTER 14

CYRIL LUCARIS—THE MAN

A T THIS POINT IT IS WORTH OUR WHILE to have a closer look at Cyril, the man, for in a short time we shall lose sight of him. He is now in his early sixties. Probably the latest picture we possess of Lucaris is the one made during the year of exile in Tenedos and which is now in Stockholm.[1] The Patriarch is portrayed as a big man, with a long beard, a serious-looking face, and thoughtful, rather melancholy eyes. In another picture, which in all probability was made two years earlier and is now to be found in the Salle Lullin of Geneva, the Patriarch is again shown as a big man with a noble face. One cannot detect, however, any trace of melancholy in his eyes, which are illumined with a lively spark which one could almost call humor. And in this, the earlier picture seems to have preserved more accurately, if not the features of the Patriarch's face, at any rate the disposition of his spirit.

For Cyril was a man gifted with a keen sense of humor, which he preserved to the very end. We have already seen how in his letter to Uytenbogaert of October 10, 1613,[2] he compares the success which the Jesuits had in Constantinople with that of foxes among poultry—"*et proficiant quot vulpes inter gallinas.*" In the same letter he gives an account of the visits which the "Jabuna," the chief of the Copts in Egypt, had paid him while he was Patriarch of Alexandria, and he can hardly restrain his mirth when he remembers the somber, long face of that silent Jabuna. "Never does one see him open his mouth, for he does not consider it permissible to a Jabuna to speak outside his own house. . . . All he does is to move his head forward or backward, as a sign of approval or disapproval of what he is being told . . . And as

for the visits he paid me, he went away as dumb as he had come
—'*quoties venit, mutus venit, mutus abiit.*' As for myself, I love
speaking—'*ego loquax et garrulus sum.*' I think it is my duty to
speak for myself and not let others do it for me. What, however,
I most dislike in that good man is that of the whole of his face he
only permits me to see his eyes; the rest he keeps covered . . . as
if by an actor's mask."

In the same letter, speaking with contempt of some of the
doctrines of the Roman Church, he says, "While the Papists teach
that no one can be certain of his salvation, they insist that the
Greeks should be certain of their damnation."

He uses his humor frequently in attacking his opponents, and
becomes quite caustic sometimes in his sarcasm. Writing to his
friend Leger on July 15, 1635,[3] from the island of Rhodes
where he is once again in exile, he remembers Athanasius Patelarus, the man who showed his gratitude to him by offering to
purchase for himself the Patriarchal dignity, and calls him, not
"Patelarus," but "that Athanasius Peshkesh, who has gone in great
haste to Rome to receive unto himself, as he says, the cardinal's
hat, which they will give him for having deposed a Calvinist
Patriarch." From the same island he gives an account of a dis-
cussion he had had on questions of theology, while in Chios, with
someone, Coressius by name, "that little genius of a theologian."[4]
Cyril's sarcasm can be easily understood and forgiven when in a
letter[5] which he penned one year before his martyrdom he called
the *Propaganda Fide* of Rome, at whose hands he had suffered so
much, "The Congregation for the Propagation of Infidelity."

This outflow of sarcasm only shows how human Cyril was—a
man of a large heart and warm disposition. He had a heart which
was always ready to forgive his enemies and to offer of the best
of its treasure to his friends. Just a short time before he was sent
into exile for the second time, he received a letter from Cyril
Contari, the man who had hurt him so deeply and who was later
to become the agent who brought about his death. Contari was in
exile in Tenedos and pretended in his letter to have repented of
the wrong he had done Lucaris, and begged him to pardon him.
Without a moment's hesitation the good Patriarch sent to this
evil man a message of full and free pardon.[6]

In an equally full measure, Cyril extended his love to his friends and to the cause for which he was fighting. To Uytenbogaert he says that he "cannot speak too much" when he speaks of religion.[7]

One cannot go through Cyril's correspondence without being struck with another beautiful trait of his personality, namely his deep and genuine humility. Cyril was by no means a common man. He had received an education which few in his time had attained. He was called to the highest offices his Church could offer him. He kept up a correspondence with the great men of his time, some of whom honored him with their friendship and others with their hatred. And it would not have been unnatural if Cyril had been conscious of his achievements and position. Such a feeling, however, is not betrayed in any of his letters. While Patriarch of Alexandria, he received a letter from Uytenbogaert in which the Dutch divine seems to have spoken warmly about the talents with which, as he was told, Cyril was endowed. In a very gracious and slightly humorous way Cyril disclaimed the possession of such talents: "And I must add, my dear sir, that as regards the talents with which you have heard that God has favored me, you must not imagine that I really possess them. I would much rather possess those I am lacking. Therefore you should attribute those good things you heard about me to the love of those who reported them to you. One must be content, however, with what God has been pleased to give him."[8]

In a letter to De Wilhem he regrets that he does not himself possess the beautiful and elegant style with which his friend's letters are embellished.[9] In the same letter he insists that De Wilhem should treat him, the Patriarch of Alexandria, with confident familiarity, and then he goes on to express his gratitude for the enlightenment he had received from De Wilhem's letters on certain truths which he had formerly ignored. Writing again to the same friend he does not hesitate to confess that his knowledge concerning the doctrine of predestination is very meager.[10]

This brings out another remarkable line in his character: his insatiable thirst for learning. Before our mind's eye we have a picture of a little Cretan boy who, after his return from Venice to his home island and while waiting for an opportunity to resume his studies in Italy, had unearthed a few books which his teacher,

Margunios, had left there. And another of a young student at the University of Padua who, during his limited leisure time, carried on a correspondence with his old teacher in which he discussed various problems of philosophy. This thirst for knowledge did not forsake Cyril to the end of his life. No sooner had he made a new friend than he asked for a loan of books. The mere names of books which he borrowed from his friends on theology, philosophy, mathematics, and the arts make an impressive list. In a letter to De Wilhem he says: *"Nihil ambio, nihil sitio, nisi ut semper aliquid discam"*—"I have no other ambition, no other desire, but always to acquire some new knowledge."[11] And to Leger he writes from Rhodes on June 25, 1635,[12] and submits a whole series of questions on various points in connection with his private study of the Bible which would suggest the quiet atmosphere of his study rather than the hardships of exile.

The knowledge which Cyril expected to gain from his studies he did not seek for his own selfish satisfaction. His aim was to use it in the service of his fellow men and thus fulfill more adequately his high office as pastor of the Church of God. "Those to whom this care is committed," he writes to Uytenbogaert,[13] "should work the work of an Evangelist and fulfill their ministry with soberness." For, he says in another letter to the same person,[14] "although both you and I are pastors, we are nevertheless subject to the Sovereign Pastor, to Whom we belong as sheep and by Whom we must be edified, if we are to be pastors."

Such was the man who for a brief space of time shone as a bright and beautiful star in the dark sky of Greece. Deeply human in his affection, conscious of his limitations and always eager to learn, humble as well as proud, full of a deep love for truth and an equally great love for his motherland, and with one great ambition and desire—to be used by God in bringing the light of the gospel to his fellow countrymen.

CHAPTER 15

THE MARTYRDOM

I T WAS IN THE SPRING OF THE YEAR 1637 that Cyril was restored to his See for the last time. It is evident from letters which he wrote during his exile[1] that he was not free from a vague feeling of fear about the future. And his friends must have realized that the enemies of the Reformation movement within the Greek Church, who had so far been frustrated in their efforts to put out of the way the chief agent of that movement, would soon be obliged to have recourse to more radical measures against him. As Smith puts it, these people, being confronted by the courageous and inflexible spirit with which Cyril had suffered exiles, imprisonments, and other hardships and had proved himself superior to all these, finally came to the conclusion that "while he lived, all hope of their plans being successful was vain."[2] It must have been early in the last term of Cyril's tenure of the office of the Patriarchate that the decision to put him to death was taken.

It is not easy to say who took the tragic initiative in this last stage in the struggle against Lucaris. Greek Orthodox writers are anxious to cast all responsibility upon the Austrian ambassador, Schwarzenhorn, thus clearing in some measure Cyril of Berroea of the ugly stain of the blame.[3] Roman Catholic historians, on the other hand, are equally anxious to lay upon Cyril Contari the whole responsibility for that crime.[4] The historical data at our disposal seem to point to both these men as being, each in his own way, responsible for bringing about Cyril's death.

A short time after Lucaris occupied the See, Cyril Contari and Schwarzenhorn began negotiations concerning the best way to bring about the removal of the hated Patriarch. Schwarzenhorn offered to intercede with the Pope and the *Propaganda* on behalf of Contari and to solicit their assistance in his efforts to supplant the Calvinist Patriarch. As a result of Schwarzenhorn's intercession, the Pope and the *Propaganda* promised to give Contari financial assistance. There seems to have been, however, some delay in the dispatch of the promised sum of money, for on October 2, 1637, Contari wrote to Schwarzenhorn to complain that the "promised friends" (that is, the money promised by the Holy See wherewith to bribe the Turkish authorities) had not yet arrived. Schwarzenhorn at once conveyed Contari's complaints to the Roman Catholic Patriarchal Vicar in Constantinople.[5] A correspondence between these two men followed in which the same mutual distrust is evident which existed at an earlier stage in Cyril's story in the relations between the French ambassador in Constantinople and Cannachio Rossi, the special envoy of the Holy See.

There followed many months of espionage, as Schwarzenhorn himself says in his report, but neither Schwarzenhorn nor Contari felt safe enough to deal the last blow against Lucaris. Their indecision was due to the fact that they were afraid that, so long as the Sultan and the Grand Vizir were in Constantinople, the English and Dutch ambassadors would find it possible to take swift measures in order to counter the intrigues of Cyril's enemies and neutralize them.[6] They decided, therefore, to bide their time, waiting for a suitable opportunity when the Sultan and the Grand Vizir would be away from Constantinople and not accessible to the English and the Dutch friends of the Patriarch.

The opportunity for which the two conspirators were waiting was not long in presenting itself. The throne of the Empire was occupied at that time by young Sultan Murad IV, under whose leadership a new breath of life blew over Turkey. Murad himself took the leadership of his army in Asia and started a campaign against the Persians which led him from victory to victory.[7] In due time he attempted the recapture of Bagdad, which was still in the hands of the Persians. When the preparations for this particular campaign were completed, the Sultan set out at the head of his army, on the eighth of May 1638, from Scutari of Constantinople, with Bagdad as his goal.[8] He was preceded by the Grand Vizir, Bairam Pasha, who had left the capital in order to prepare the way in Asia Minor for his royal master and his large army. This was the opportunity for which Contari and Schwarzen-horn had waited patiently for so many months.

They immediately dispatched to Asia Minor a Greek priest, by the name of Lamerno, with instructions to make contact with the Grand Vizir, now that he was at a safe distance from Constantin-ople and Cyril's friends. If we might make a conjecture from the timetable of the Sultan's course through Asia Minor, the meeting of Lamerno with the Grand Vizir must have taken place near the town of Konia, the ancient Iconium.[9] And the meeting was made possible by means of rich presents, with which the Grand Vizir was bribed. This is testified by Smith,[10] who, in his chapter on Cyril's death, bases his account on Nathaniel Conopius' narrative —of which we shall presently speak—as well as on information which he received from Edward Pococke, professor of Arabic in Oxford, who at the time of Lucaris' death was chaplain to the English ambassador in Constantinople.

It seems that Lamerno stayed at the place where he had his audience with the Grand Vizir long enough to be able to send to Constantinople reports of his proceedings even before the sen-tence of death was actually issued. Thus Schwarzenhorn in his report says of Contari: "After a few days we were again together and the Patriarch whispered in my ear: 'My agent writes from Asia that Lucaris will have some difficulty in escaping death; what do you think of that?' I answered him that to my mind the Patriarch ought to do nothing, one way or another, but to let things take their course. The Patriarch then smiled and never again spoke to me on this subject."[11]

At last the efforts of Lamerno were crowned with success. The Grand Vizir had an opportunity to approach the Sultan on the matter of Lucaris, choosing very cleverly the grounds on which to rouse his suspicions. In this, the famous Cossacks proved once again useful. The joy which the victories over the Persians had brought to the hearts of all was somewhat mitigated at about this time by the news that Asak, a town on the sea of Azov, had been besieged and captured by the Cossacks.[12] This was a blow for Murad, all the more bitter because, being occupied with the Persian campaign, he could not avenge it immediately. At this critical time, when even the slightest allusion to the Cossacks would be sure to infuriate Murad, the Grand Vizir made the insinuation to the Sultan that the Greek Patriarch had a hand in the fall of Asak. Our authorities are not clear about the share in the fall of that town imputed to Cyril. It was stated to the Sultan, however, that Cyril had been keeping a secret correspondence with the Moscovites and the Cossacks, and furthermore it was suggested that Cyril's presence in Constantinople was dangerous at a time when the army was away, as he might incite the Greek population to revolt.[13] That was enough for Murad. Under such circumstances even a more sober and controlled person might have found it difficult to restrain himself. But Murad IV, now at the age of twenty-six, had already built up for himself a great record of crime and had won for himself the title of "the Nero of Turkey."[14]

He was "half-Greek," because his mother was Greek, and his favorite wife was also Greek.[15] He came to the throne in 1623, and at the time of Cyril's death he had already committed a large number of his famous crimes, among which was the murder of his three brothers.[16] In 1637 the number of his victims, many of whom he had executed with his own hand, was estimated at about twenty-five thousand.[17] It is said that one could trace the route he took in his campaign for the recapture of Bagdad by the red line he left behind him—the blood of governors of provinces, judges, and other officials whom he had executed.[18] Shortly after he had sentenced Cyril to death, he committed the most horrible of all his crimes, when, at the capture of Bagdad, he put to death the whole of that town's garrison, consisting of thirty thousand men, as well as a great number of its citizens. Such was the terror which he inspired in those around him that, as Ranke puts it, "his mutes were no longer to be distinguished from the other slaves of the Palace, for they all conversed now by signs."[19]

"It is not to be wondered at," to use the words of the historian Von Hammer, "if that blood-thirsty tyrant . . . did not respect the saintly character of the Pastor of the Greek Church."[20] The sentence which condemned the Patriarch of Constantinople to death was passed and dispatched in all haste by special messenger to the Caimacam, the governor of the city in the absence of the Grand Vizir, with the order to have it executed immediately.[21]

The Caimacam, Musa Pasha, dispatched an officer and four soldiers to the residence of the Patriarch. They seized Cyril and brought him to the Prison of the Seven Towers, on the western coast of the Bosphorus, near the Black Sea. We cannot say with accuracy how long he was kept there as a prisoner. Conopius' account might lead one to believe that he was left there only for a few hours.[22] Allatius, however, says that Cyril's execution occurred a few days—"*paucis diebus*"—after his imprisonment,[23] and Schwarzenhorn in his report to the Emperor says that the execution took place five days after the imprisonment.[24] We know, however, that in the evening of June 27, 1638, another detachment of soldiers came to the castle to lead Cyril to the place of execution. Fearing lest the news should spread in the city and arouse the people to a sedition, the officer in charge told Cyril that they had orders to take him by boat to the port of St. Stephanos in the south of Constantinople, where he would be embarked on a ship for a new place of exile. However, as soon as the boat set sail, Cyril perceived that he was being led not into exile but to his death. He therefore knelt down in the boat and offered his last prayer to the Lord he had served so faithfully.[25]

It was twilight when the boat reached a solitary point on the coast near St. Stephanos and the detachment of the soldiers landed, together with their prisoner. And as the sun was going down on that memorable day of the twenty-seventh of June, 1638, the last command was given and the Patriarch was executed. The man at the head of the detachment passed the noose round the Patriarch's throat and strangled him. Thus did Cyril Lucaris meet his end at the age of sixty-six.[26] The body of the Patriarch was buried by the soldiers near the beach and, in accordance with the custom prevailing at the time, his belongings were distributed among the soldiers, who on the following day sold them in the market place of the city.

That is how the terrible news broke out in the city. At once crowds of mourning people were assembled outside Contari's residence, shouting: "Pilate, give unto us the body of our dead one, that we may bury him." From Contari's house the crowd proceeded to the residence of the Caimacam, to whom they offered money so that he might give them the dead body of their pastor. But Contari and his friends, who were afraid even of the dead body of Lucaris, persuaded the Caimacam to refuse the request of the people. A few days later they sent their servants to the place of Cyril's execution, to have his body dug out of the grave and cast into the sea. Some fishermen, however, who saw the body floating on the sea, recognized it and brought it to the little island of St. Andrew, not far from Constantinople, on the Asiatic coast, where they buried it.[27]

The news was sent to the *Propaganda* in Rome by the Austrian ambassador, in a letter dated August 1, 1638,[28] where Schwarzenhorn speaks of two previous letters by which he had announced the news of Cyril's imprisonment. These letters are, no doubt, to be found in the archives of the *Propaganda* in Rome, and they might possibly shed more light on the events which took place in the last days of Lucaris' life. Unfortunately, they were not published by Hofmann together with the others.

In his letter Schwarzenhorn can hardly suppress his joy: "Thus the wretched existence of that unfortunate old man received, by the just intervention of Divine Providence, its fitting retribution, through his shameful and miserable death." In his report to the Emperor he says: "As for me, I must admit that Lucaris' death did not displease me, for he was the chief assistant of the Dutch Ambassador in his frequent interventions with the Porte."[29]

Contari, the chief agent in Cyril's tragic death, was not left to enjoy his triumph for long. Soon after Sultan Murad's return to Constantinople, in June 1639, he was deposed and sent into exile to Carthage, where he met with a miserable death.[30] And Lamerno, in order to avoid a similar end, became a renegade.

Contari was succeeded on the Ecumenical Throne by Parthenius I, who was a friend of Lucaris, and under him the Church had an opportunity to pay a belated tribute of honor to the memory of the great Patriarch. In 1641 the remains of Cyril's body were taken from the island of St. Andrew and were buried in the Monastery of the Holy Virgin on the island of Halke. The funeral service which took place in the Church of the Patriarchate was a solemn ceremony and was attended by a great number of the people of the royal city, who came to honor the memory of the Patriarch.[31]

But the real farewell of Greece to the man who in her darkest hours loved her, worked for her, and at last laid down his life for her, was expressed in that simple act of devotion when the rough hands of workingmen dug a solitary grave on the shore of St. Andrew and there deposited the remains of Cyril Lucaris.

☐ CHAPTER 16

ACHIEVEMENTS AND ASSESSMENTS

THERE REMAINS FOR US NOW to attempt to assess the measure of success which attended the work of Cyril Lucaris, and, should we find it to be small, to inquire into the reasons for this.

It need hardly be pointed out that Lucaris' work had no great measure of success. The fact that some of his admirers today find it necessary, as has been shown in an earlier chapter, to dissociate Lucaris from his work by refusing him the authorship of the *Confessio,* and thus to clear his memory from the stain of the Reformation, is sufficient evidence that Lucaris' work made little impression on the minds of his people. It would be unjust, however, to say that it had no effect whatever on the life of his country and that with the passing of Lucaris his work vanished as well.

We should consider first of all the handful of people who were influenced by Lucaris' work and embraced his message. First in our list comes Meletios Pantogalos, the Archbishop of Ephesus. Pantogalos fully shared the evangelical beliefs of Lucaris. In a letter to the clergy of Crete, Pantogalos calls Cyril "the good Pastor and wise Captain of the Church." As regards the *Confessio,* he says that the people who reject it are those who are unable to enter into its full meaning. And he asks: "Were not our Fathers Athanasius, Basil and Chrysostom called heretics by the heretics themselves?"[1] Father Simon, in his *Critical History of the Religions and Customs of the Eastern Nations,* mentions a letter of Pantogalos to certain divines at Leyden, in which he rejects the veneration of the saints, the doctrine of transubstantiation, the worship of the icons, etc. "We declare," he says, "that it is not permissible for one to hold any of the above doctrines, nor any other human doctrine, but only what has been given us by our Lord and His inspired Apostles."[2]

Pantogalos seems to have been a good preacher. Before he was made a bishop, he was sent by Lucaris as a missionary to preach in various provinces of his Church. On that occasion Cyril addressed a circular letter to all the clergy and to other Christian people in the provinces, in which he likens Pantogalos to a good doctor. And he goes on to say that when a good doctor is found, it is not fitting that he should be confined to one place, but all people should have access to him. And as Pantogalos was a good doctor, "he is now sent to travel in all provinces, East and West, to teach the people the doctrines of the Gospel."[3]

Next comes Nathaniel Conopius, a priest and follower of Lucaris, to whom we are indebted for an account of the details of the Patriarch's martyrdom. Conopius, too, was a Cretan. After Cyril's death, we find him in Oxford, a student in Balliol College. John Evelyn mentions him in his Diary as "a fellow-commoner" of his. He refers to him as the student who came "from Cyril, the Patriarch of Constantinople"; and what seems to have impressed Evelyn particularly was that "he was the first I ever saw drink coffee; which custom came not into England till thirty years after."[4] When Conopius left Oxford, he continued his studies at the University of Leyden.[5] While in Leyden, Conopius expressed the desire to translate Calvin's *Institutiones* into Modern Greek,[6] and according to A. Demetracopoulos[7] he did so.[8]

We have already mentioned in an earlier chapter Neophytus, the Archbishop of Heracleia, as being a follower of Lucaris. The same can be said of Parthenius the Younger, who succeeded Cyril Contari to the Ecumenical Throne.[9] To these must be added Sophronius, Bishop of Athens, about whom Lucaris himself in writing to Leger on the tenth of March, 1637, says: "He is one of my friends, with very good intentions towards the Reformed Religion";[10] the monk Maximus Callioupolites, who as we have seen was a valued collaborator of Lucaris in one of the two great works of his life; and Philip the Cypriot, a dignitary of the Church of Constantinople, who seems to have taken an active part in the translation of the New Testament and therefore provoked severe censure from Archimandrite Arsenios of Vlachia.

These are the people we know who were influenced by Lucaris' message and who openly declared themselves in favor of his work of reformation. To these we might probably add a few more, whose names have not come down to us. But even after the addition of these unknown followers the number is disappointingly small. If we were to judge the work of Lucaris by the number of his avowed followers then we might say, without any doubt, that it had very little success.

The extent of the success of Lucaris' effort for reformation should not, however, be measured by the number of his followers, small or large. We should rather look for its success in another direction, in which his work had a lasting influence on his people. This is the first edition of the New Testament in Modern Greek, to which we have already referred in a previous chapter. With this edition in his hand the Patriarch sowed in the hearts of his people the first seeds of the religious reformation which sooner or later brought its fruit.

The advice which Lucaris gave to his people in the preface of this book, where he exhorts them not to neglect to profit by the reading "of the translated sacred and holy Gospel," was not given in vain. For we have proof that this first Modern Greek New Testament helped to increase the interest of the Greek people in the Scriptures. Forty years after the death of Lucaris, Paul Ricaut, formerly English Consul in Smyrna, states that the Scriptures were read in the churches "in the Vulgar Tongue."[11] It should be noted that Ricaut was by no means a sympathizer of Lucaris and strongly disapproved of this reading of the Scriptures "in the Vulgar Tongue." Therefore his testimony is all the more valuable. We do not know how widespread this practice of having the Scriptures read in public worship, in the translation provided by Lucaris, was in Ricaut's time, nor how long it lasted, as it eventually died out; but we do know that while it lasted it was an influence for good.

That is as far as we can trace the influence of the work of Lucaris on the Greek people. We should be careful not to minimize it. Such as it was, it was good. When placed, however, beside the work of the Reformers of the sixteenth century in other countries, we have to admit that it seems small and insignificant. And we feel the need to inquire into the reasons for this.

The Reformation movement of the sixteenth century was not a fact which leaped into being unheralded and unprepared. It was a complex movement for which many forces were at work, preparing the way for it, long before it made its appearance in history. We can distinguish at least four main factors, operating in the West, each one of which made its contribution to the preparation of that religious upheaval which we call the Reformation. These are the political, the social, the intellectual, and the religious factors. And all four were either entirely or almost non-existent in the Greek East when Lucaris appeared on the scene of public life.

In connection with the political factor, we should note the rise of the national state before the time of the Reformation, making it possible for the sovereigns of various states in Europe to give the movement their support even though they were not actually interested in it; for, as it has been said, "there was no assistance so much desired . . . in their disputes with the Popes, as that of a spiritual opposition to their decrees."[12]

Such a state of things did not exist in the Greek East previous to, or during, the time when Lucaris began his work in the Greek Church. The only political influence to be mentioned as having had any bearing on Lucaris' work, was the antagonism in the Near East between England and Holland on the one hand, and France on the other. This antagonism was in some measure responsible for the protection given to Lucaris by the ambassadors of the two Protestant countries.

Besides the political factor, there was also the social factor operating in the West before the actual appearance of the Reformation movement. The *Bundschuh,* a strongly anticlerical movement in Germany, is only one instance of various other similar movements which broke out in various countries in the West, and which aimed to vindicate the rights of the people as against the oppression of the clergy. It was the activity of the *Bundschuh* in Germany at that time which, as has been said, made that country "the most favorable place that Luther could have chosen for his birth."[13]

Such a social movement did not and probably could not exist or, at any rate, make itself felt in the Greek East at the time of Lucaris. The nation was then in a state of slavery, and the Church was not only an ecclesiastical power, but was also its only national authority. An uprising, therefore, against the oppression of their clergy would only harm the national interests of the Greeks at that time.

It is somewhat misleading, however, to speak of the oppression of the clergy in connection with the Greek Church of that period. The Greek clergy had by no means developed that power which in the West was exerting so vast an influence in the life of the people. The chief complaint which could be brought against the clergy of the Greek Church at that time is that, far from exerting an unduly oppressive influence, it exercised no influence at all, for lack of even an elementary education among the majority of its members. And this brings us to the third, the intellectual factor.

It is a tragic irony that the country which probably made the greatest contribution to this factor was herself bereft of its fruits. The Greek scholars who came to the West, after the fall of Constantinople, bringing with them the precious texts of the classical authors, had a great share in initiating the movement of the Renaissance. This movement, with the impetus which it gave to the study of the Scriptures in the original languages, and with the spirit of reaction which it cultivated against the tyranny of tradition that had firmly imposed itself upon the life of the Church, constituted the first shock which the edifice of the Church of Rome received before the actual earthquake of the Reformation came upon it. And when the discovery of the art of printing made it possible for the knowledge heretofore possessed by the few to be communicated to the masses, the minds of the people were prepared to listen to and receive the message of the Reformation.

Such was the state of the intellectual life of the people in the West. And it was a picture in absolute contrast to that which the Greek East had to offer. Since the fall of Constantinople, Greece had suffered a double loss: the exodus of her scholars to the lands of the West and the terrible system of "child-gathering," which was systematically and ruthlessly enforced by the Turks. And the effects of this double loss were only too visible in the intellectual life of the people. It may not be an exaggeration to say that Greece never knew a more sterile period in her history than the time when the Renaissance and, later, the Reformation were stirring the lands of the West into a new life.

And last to be considered is the religious factor. Before the coming of Luther and the other Reformers, the ground was being prepared by various religious movements. In Germany and England, in France and Italy, the message of the Reformation had been given to the people long before the Reformers appeared. As it has been well said, "The people was waiting for its prophet, and when the prophet appeared . . . he found a generation ready to respond and rally to his side."[14] Thus we find that in the country of the chief of the Reformers the minds of the people had been largely prepared by the "Friends of God," as well as by the "Brethren of the Common Life," through their preaching and the religious literature which they published and spread abroad. The extent of Luther's debt to the "Friends of God" can be seen in the preface which he supplied to the second edition of the famous *Theologia Germanica*—the masterpiece of this movement, which appeared long before Luther was born—in which he states: "I will say, though it be boastful of myself, and I speak as a fool, that next to the Bible and St. Augustine, no book hath ever come into my hands, whence I learned or could learn more of what God and Christ and man and all things are."

At the same time the Lollards were arousing the people in England and Scotland. The force of their preaching was so strongly felt by the official Church that the Archbishop of Canterbury complained to the Bishop of London that " certain unauthorized persons are setting forth erroneous, yea, heretical assertions in public sermons," while in Scotland, in 1416, all masters of the University of St. Andrews were under obligation to defend the Church to the utmost of their powers against the attacks of the Lollards.[15]

Movements of a positively spiritual nature antagonistic to the Church appeared in France and Italy as early as in the twelfth century in the form of the "Poor Men of Lyons" and of the "Cathari." The persecutions which these movements suffered from the thirteenth to the end of the fifteenth century are evidence of the degree to which they were considered to be a danger to the existing ecclesiastical system.

Shortly before the Reformation, preaching was revived in the West. Preachers were provided with new material, such as the *Biblia Pauperum,* the *Postilla,* and others. And the place which preaching was now gaining in the life of the Church was such that certain distinguished churchmen used to say that it was even more important than saying Mass.[16] It was about this same time that the Scriptures appeared in the vernacular of most countries of western Europe, and with the help of the printing press were finding their way to the hands of the people. No less than fourteen versions of the whole Bible had been printed in High German and three in Low German before Luther produced his own translation.

All these factors of religious awakening, which paved the way in the West for the coming of the Reformation, were undreamt of in the Greek East. As has been stated in an earlier chapter, preaching as a part of the church ritual had been dead for so long that the pulpit, even as a piece of furniture, had disappeared in Lucaris' time. And the first New Testament in the vernacular of the people did not make its appearance until the year of the death of the Patriarch.

Considering the fact that the above-mentioned factors, as powers preparing the ground for the work of the Reformation, were almost nonexistent in Greece, it will not be surprising that the work of Cyril Lucaris did not achieve a large measure of success. It could be said of Lucaris that he was a man born before his time. He came to labor in a field which had received no preparation whatsoever. Lucaris, therefore, cannot be called a Reformer in the strict sense of the term. He was, however, a forerunner of the Reformation movement among his people, and it was he who placed the first stone in the edifice of the religious life of modern Greece.

APPENDIX

EASTERN CONFESSION OF THE CHRISTIAN FAITH
(An English Translation)

*In the name of the Father and of the Son
and of the Holy Ghost*

Cyril, Patriarch of Constantinople, publishes this brief Confession for the benefit of those who inquire about the faith and the religion of the Greeks, that is of the Eastern Church, in witness to God and to men and with a sincere conscience without any dissimulation.

CHAPTER 1. We believe in one God, true, Almighty, and in three persons, Father, Son, and Holy Ghost; the Father unbegotten, the Son begotten of the Father before the world, consubstantial with the Father; the Holy Ghost proceeding from the Father by the Son, having the same essence with the Father and the Son. We call these three persons in one essence the Holy Trinity, ever to be blessed, glorified, and worshiped by every creature.

CHAPTER 2. We believe the Holy Scripture to be given by God, to have no other author but the Holy Ghost. This we ought undoubtedly to believe, for it is written: We have a more sure word of prophecy, to which ye do well to take heed, as to a light shining in a dark place. We believe the authority of the Holy Scripture to be above the authority of the Church. To be taught by the Holy Ghost is a far different thing from being taught by a man; for man may through ignorance err, deceive and be deceived, but the Word of God neither deceiveth nor is deceived, nor can err, and is infallible and has eternal authority.

CHAPTER 3. We believe that the most merciful God hath predestinated His elect unto glory before the beginning of the world, without any respect unto their works and that there was no other impulsive cause to this election, but only the good will and mercy of God. In like manner before the world was made, He hath rejected whom He would, of which act of reprobation, if you consider the absolute dealing of God, His will is the cause; but if you look upon the laws and principles of good order, which God's providence is making use of in the government of the world, His justice is the cause, for God is merciful and just.

CHAPTER 4. We believe that one God in Trinity, the Father, Son, and Holy Ghost, to be the Creator of all things visible and invisible. Invisible things we call the angels, visible things we call the heavens and all things under them. And because the Creator is good by nature, He hath created all things good, and He cannot do any evil; and if there be any evil, it proceedeth either from the Devil or from man. For it ought to be a certain rule to us, that God is not the Author of evil, neither can sin by any just reason be imputed to Him.

CHAPTER 5. We believe that all things are governed by God's providence, which we ought rather to adore than to search into. Since it is beyond our capacity, neither can we truly understand the reason of it from the things themselves, in which matter we suppose it better to embrace silence in humility than to speak many things which do not edify.

CHAPTER 6. We believe that the first man created by God fell in Paradise, because he neglected the commandment of God and yielded to the deceitful counsel of the serpent. From thence sprung up original sin to his posterity, so that no man is born according to the flesh who does not bear this burden and feel the fruits of it in his life.

CHAPTER 7. We believe that Jesus Christ our Lord emptied Himself, that is He assumed man's nature into His own substance. That He was conceived by the Holy Ghost in the womb of the ever virgin Mary, was born, suffered death, was buried, and risen in glory, that He might bring salvation and glory to all believers, Whom we look for to come to judge both quick and dead.

CHAPTER 8. We believe that our Lord Jesus Christ sitteth on the right hand of His Father and there He maketh intercession for us, executing alone the office of a true and lawful high priest and mediator, and from thence He hath the care of His people and governeth His Church adorning and enriching her with many blessings.

CHAPTER 9. We believe that without faith no man can be saved. And we call faith that which justifieth in Christ Jesus, which the life and death of our Lord Jesus Christ procured, the Gospel published, and without which no man can please God.

CHAPTER 10. We believe that the Church, which is called catholic, containeth all true believers in Christ, those who having departed their country are in heaven and those who live on earth are yet on the way.

The Head of which Church (because a mortal man by no means can be) Jesus Christ is alone, and holdeth the rudder of the government of the Church in His own hand. Because, however, there are on earth particular visible Churches, every one of them hath one chief, who is not properly to be called a head of that particular Church, but improperly, because he is the principal member thereof.

CHAPTER 11. We believe that the members of the Catholic Church are the saints, chosen unto eternal life, from the number and fellowship of whom hypocrites are excluded, though in particular visible Churches tares may be found amongst the wheat.

CHAPTER 12. We believe that the Church on earth is sanctified and instructed by the Holy Ghost, for He is the true comforter, whom Christ sendeth from the Father to teach the truth and to expel darkness from the understanding of the faithful. For it is true and certain that the Church on earth may err, choosing falsehood instead of truth, from which error the light and doctrine of the Holy Spirit alone freeth us, not of mortal man, although by mediation of the labors of the faithful ministers of the Church this may be done.

CHAPTER 13. We believe that man is justified by faith and not by works. But when we say by faith, we understand the correlative or object of faith, which is the righteousness of Christ, which, as if by a hand, faith apprehends and applieth unto us for our salvation. This we say without any prejudice to good works, for truth itself teacheth us that works must not be neglected, that they are necessary means to testify to our faith and confirm our calling. But that works are sufficient for our salvation, that they can enable one to appear before the tribunal of Christ and that of their own merit they can confer salvation, human frailty witnesseth to be false; but the righteousness of Christ being applied to the penitent, doth alone justify and save the faithful.

CHAPTER 14. We believe that free will is dead in the unregenerate, because they can do no good thing, and whatsoever they do is sin; but in the regenerate by the grace of the Holy Spirit the will is excited and in deed worketh but not without the assistance of grace. In order, therefore, that man should be born again and do good, it is necessary that grace should go before; otherwise man is wounded having received as many wounds as that man received who going from Jerusalem down to Jericho fell into the hands of thieves, so that of himself he cannot do anything.

CHAPTER 15. We believe that the Evangelical Sacraments in the Church are those which the Lord hath instituted in the Gospel, and they are two; these only have been delivered unto us and He who instituted them delivered unto us no more. Furthermore, we believe that they consist of the Word and the Element, that they are the seals of the promises of God, and they do confer grace. But that the Sacrament be entire and whole, it is requisite that an earthly substance and an external action concur with the use of that element ordained by Christ our Lord and joined with a true faith, because the defect of faith prejudiceth the integrity of the Sacrament.

CHAPTER 16. We believe that Baptism is a Sacrament instituted by the Lord, and unless a man hath received it, he hath no communion with Christ, from whose death, burial, and glorious resurrection the whole virtue and efficacy of Baptism doth proceed; therefore, we are certain that to those who are baptized in the same form which our Lord hath commanded in the Gospel, both original and actual sins are pardoned, so that whosoever hath been washed in the name of the Father and of the Son and of the Holy Ghost are regenerate, cleansed, and justified. But concerning the repetition of it, we have no command to be rebaptized, therefore we must abstain from this indecent thing.

CHAPTER 17. We believe that the other Sacrament which was ordained by the Lord is that which we call Eucharist. For in the night in which the Lord offered up Himself, He took bread and blessed it and He said to the Apostles, "Take ye, eat, this is my body"; and when He had taken the cup, He gave thanks and said, "Drink ye all of this, this is my blood which was shed for many; this do in remembrance of me." And Paul addeth, "For as often as ye shall eat of this bread and drink of this cup, ye do shew the Lord's death." This is the pure and lawful institution of this wonderful Sacrament, in the administration of which we profess the true and certain presence of our Lord Jesus Christ; that presence, however, which faith offereth to us, not that which the devised doctrine of transubstantiation teacheth. For we believe that the faithful do eat the body of Christ in the Supper of the Lord, not by breaking it with the teeth of the body, but by perceiving it with the sense and feeling of the soul, since the body of Christ is not that which is visible in the Sacrament, but that which faith spiritually apprehendeth and offereth to us; from whence it is true that, if we believe, we do eat and partake, if we do not believe, we are destitute of all the fruit of it. We believe, consequently, that to drink the cup in the Sacrament is to be partaker of the true blood of our Lord Jesus Christ, in the same manner as we affirmed of the body; for as the Author of it commanded concerning His body, so He did concerning His blood; which commandment ought neither to be dismembered nor maimed, according to the fancy of man's arbitrament; yea rather the institution ought to be kept as it was delivered to us. When therefore we have been partakers of the body and blood of Christ worthily and have communicated entirely, we acknowledge ourselves to be reconciled, united to our

Head of the same body, with certain hope to be co-heirs in the Kingdom to come.

CHAPTER 18. We believe that the souls of the dead are either in blessedness or in damnation, according as every one hath done, for as soon as they move out of the body they pass either to Christ or into hell; for as a man is found at his death, so he is judged, and after this life there is neither power nor opportunity to repent; in this life there is a time of grace, they therefore who be justified here shall suffer no punishment hereafter; but they who die, being not justified, are appointed for everlasting punishment. By which it is evident that the fiction of Purgatory is not to be admitted but in the truth it is determined that every one ought to repent in this life and to obtain remission of his sins by our Lord Jesus Christ, if he will be saved. And let this be the end.

This brief Confession of ours we conjecture will be a sign spoken against them who are pleased to slander and persecute us. But we trust in the Lord Jesus Christ and hope that He will not relinquish the cause of His faithful ones, nor let the rod of wickedness lie upon the lot of the righteous.

Dated in Constantinople in the month of March 1629.

CYRIL, Patriarch of Constantinople

▣ FOOTNOTES

CHAPTER 1

EARLY YEARS

(1) Lucaris, according to a note by Archbishop Laud, mentioned in Thomas Smith's *Collectanea de Cyrillo Lucaris,* p. 65, was born about 1558. But the most probable date of his birth, generally accepted, is November 13, 1572. See Antoine Leger, "Fragmentum Vitae" in Smith's *Collectanea,* p. 77.

(2) For details about his life see Nicolaos Comnenos Papadopolus, *Historia Gymnasii Patavini,* Vol. II, pp. 264-265.

(3) Ὕμνοι Ἀνακρεόντειοι, *cum interpretatione Latina Conradi Rittershusii. Augustae. Ex oficina typographica Joan. Praetorii. Anno S. N. MDCI.*

(4) A. Legrand, *Bibliographie Hellénique du XVII Siècle,* Vol. IV, pp. 177-178. See his letter to Lucaris, Venice, June 9, 1589.

(5) *Ibid.,* letter of July 22, 1589, pp. 188-190.

(6) *Ibid.,* letter of June 19, 1589, pp. 180-181 and letter of July 8, 1589, pp. 182-183.

(7) *Ibid.,* letter of Nicolaos Rhodios, October 27, 1590, pp. 202-203.

(8) As quoted by Alethea Wiel, *Venice,* pp. 311-312.

(9) George Sandys, *A Relation of a Journey Begun An. Dom. 1610,* p. 2. London, 1627.

(10) Lacy Collison-Morley, *Italy after the Renaissance,* p. 222; A. J. Grant, *A History of Europe from 1494 to 1610,* pp. 67-68; A. H. Johnson, *Europe in the 16th Century,* p. 88; J. A. Crowe and G. B. Cavalcaselle, *Titian: His Life and Times,* Vol. I, pp. 1-24 *passim.*

(11) J. E. Sandys, *History of Classical Scholarship,* Vol. II, p. 79.

(12) Ἐτυμολογικὸν Μέγα κατὰ ἀλφάβητον, Venetiis, 1499.

(13) See Ambroise Firmin-Didot, *Alde et l'Hellénisme à Vénise,* pp. 435-437.

(14) Leopold von Ranke, *History of the Popes in the 16th and 17th Centuries,* Vol. II, pp. 114-115.

(15) Wiel, *op. cit.,* p. 375.

(16) See Arnold Junn, *Venice,* pp. 35-39; Wiel, *op. cit.,* p. 160.

(17) Philarete Chasles, *Galileo Galilei,* p. 28.

CHAPTER 2

BACK IN CRETE

(1) Thomas Dallam, *The Diary of Master Thomas Dallam, 1599-1600,* published in the Volume of the Hakluyt Society, p. 26. London, 1893; George Sandys, *Relation of a Journey Begun An. Dom. 1610,* pp. 222-223.

(2) William Miller, *Essays on the Latin Orient,* pp. 177-178.

(3) S. Xanthudides, *The Venetians in Crete and the Struggles of the Cretans,* pp. 126-127, 159-160. Athens, 1939; Miller, *op. cit.,* pp. 179-180.

(4) Miller, *op. cit.*, p. 177.

(5) Xanthudides, *op. cit.*, pp. 161-163.

(6) *Ibid.*, p. 162.

(7) Legrand, *Bibliographie Hellénique du XVII Siècle*, Vol. II, p. 395.

(8) *Ibid.*, letter of October 2, 1611, Vol. IV, p. 268.

(9) *Ibid.*, letter of April 2, 1611, p. 266.

(10) *Ibid.*, letter to Ecumenical Patriarch Timothy of June 4, 1613, p. 279.

(11) *Ibid.*, letter of July 6, 1594, p. 215.

(12) Papadopolus, *Historia Gymnasii Patavini*, Vol. II, pp. 292-293.

(13) Legrand, *op. cit.*, letter of June 9, 1589, Vol. IV, pp. 177-178.

(14) *Ibid.*, letters of March 8, 1589, June 9, 1589, another one of the same date, June 19, 1589, pp. 175-177, 177-178, 178-179, 180-181.

CHAPTER 3

A STUDENT IN PADUA

(1) Legrand, *Bibliographie Hellénique du XVII Siècle*, Vol. IV, pp. 177-178.

(2) Rashdall, *Medieval Universities*, Vol. II, pp. 9-21.

(3) Papadopolus, *Historia Gymnasii Patavini*, Vol. II, pp. 121-122.

(4) *Ibid.*, pp. 42-44, 98-100, 132-135, 177.

(5) Firmin-Didot, *Alde et l'Hellénisme à Vénise*, p. 461.

(6) Papadopolus, *op. cit.*, Vol. I, pp. 339-340.

(7) *Ibid.*, pp. 359-361.

(8) *Ibid.*

(9) Rashdall, *op. cit.*, p. 21.

(10) Legrand, *op. cit.*, pp. 193-194.

(11) Francis Marion Crawford, *Gleanings from Venetian History*, pp. 574-579.

(12) Legrand, *op. cit.*, pp. 193-194.

(13) *Ibid.*, p. 195.

(14) *Ibid.*, pp. 190-192, 192-193.

(15) D'Arcy Power, *William Harvey*, pp. 14-26.

(16) Legrand, *op. cit.*, pp. 214-215.

CHAPTER 4

MISSION TO POLAND

(1) Smith, *Collectanea*, p. 7; Leger, "Fragmentum Vitae," in Smith's *Collectanea*, p. 77; Father Simon, *The Critical History of the Religions and Customs of the Eastern Nations*, English translation by A. Lovell, p. 46 (1685), places the ordination before the studies in Padua. He gives no authority. Chrysostom Papadopoulos, *Cyril Lucaris*, p. 15, Athens, 1939, states that Cyril was ordained in Crete a deacon in 1592 and the following year a priest. He gives no authorities.

(2) A. Pichler, *Geshichte des Protestantismus in der Orientalischen Kirche in 17 Jahrhundert*, pp. 61-66, (1862); Le Quien, *Oriens Christianus*, Vol. II, p. 265; Kimmel, *Monumenta Fidei Ecclesiae Orientalis*, p. XXIV, (1750).

(3) Smith, *op. cit.*, p. 7.

(4) All the above authorities.

(5) Cf. B. J. Kidd, *The Counter-Reformation*, pp. 221-223, and Von Ranke, *History of the Popes in the 16th and 17th Centuries*, English translation, Vol. II, pp. 137-139.

(6) Kidd, *op. cit.*, pp. 221-223.

(7) Von Ranke, *op. cit.*, p. 82.

(8) Thomas Griesinger, *The Jesuits*, pp. 275-277; Kidd, *op. cit.*, pp. 221-223.

(9) Von Ranke, *op. cit.*, pp. 137-142.

(10) Smith, *op. cit.*, p. 9; Von Ranke, *op. cit.*, p. 142.

(11) Smith, *op. cit.*, pp. 10-13; Leger, *op. cit.*, p. 78; G. Hofmann, S. J., "Patriarch Kyrillos Lucaris und die Romische Kirche," in *Orientalia Christiana*, p. 9, May 1929.

(12) Smith, *op. cit.*, p. 9; Von Ranke, *op. cit.*, Vol. II, p. 142.

(13) Smith, *op. cit.*, p. 10.

(14) Legrand, *Bibliographie Hellénique du XVII Siècle*, Vol. IV, pp. 225-227.

(15) *Ibid.*, p. 221.

(16) *Ibid.*, pp. 225-227, 228-229.

(17) Leger, *op. cit.*, p. 78.

(18) Papadopoulos, *op. cit.*, p. 21.

(19) Legrand, *op. cit.*, p. 221.

(20) A. P. Kerameus, *Greek Texts Useful for the Study of the History of Rumania*, p. 416.

(21) Legrand, *op. cit.*, p. 217.

(22) *Ibid.*, pp. 229-230.

(23) *Ibid.*, p. 220.

(24) *Ibid.*, pp. 228-229.

(25) Leger, *op. cit.*, pp. 78-79.

(26) *Ibid.*, p. 79. About the duration of Cyril's stay with Constantine Basil there seems to be some confusion.

(27) Legrand, *op. cit.*, p. 220.

(28) *Codex of Metochium of Holy Sepulchre in Constantinople*, No. 408, pp. 44-49.

(29) Smith, *op. cit.*, p. 11.

(30) Legrand, *op. cit.*, p. 215.

(31) Agathangelos Ninolaki, *Meletios Pegas*, p. 165; C. Sathas, *Modern Greek Literature*, p. 209.

(32) Leger, *op. cit.*, pp. 79-80; Smith, *op. cit.*, p. 12.

(33) Smith, *op. cit.*, p. 13.

(34) Papadopoulos, *op. cit.*, p. 27.

(35) *Codex of Metochium, op. cit.*, pp. 58, 73, 81, 84.

(36) Leger, *op. cit.*, p. 80.

CHAPTER 5

PATRIARCH OF ALEXANDRIA

(1) Leger, "Fragmentum Vitae," in Smith's *Collectanea*, p. 80. Smith himself, in his *Collectanea*, p. 13, places this event in 1602 or 1603.

(2) J. M. Neale, *History of the Holy Eastern Church; Patriarchate of Alexandria*, Vol. II, p. 358.

(3) John Covel, *Some Account of the Present Greek Church*, Preface, p. xi, Cambridge, 1722.

(4) J. Aymon, *Monumens Authentiques de la Religion de Grèce* (1708). His letter to Uytenbogaert, October 10, 1613, p. 152.

(5) G. Mazarakes, *Metrophanes Critopoulos*, pp. 59-69.

(6) Aymon, *op. cit.*, p. 157.

(7) *Ibid.*, pp. 188-192.

(8) De la Croix, *La Turquie Chrétienne sous la Pussiante Protection de Louis le Grand*, 1695, p. 153.

(9) Sandys, *Relation of a Journey Begun An. Dom. 1610*, pp. 114-115.

(10) *Ibid.*, pp. 119-126, *passim*.

(11) Philippus Cyprius, Χρονικὸν τῆς Ἑλληνικῆς Ἐκκλησίας, p. 447 (1679).

(12) Legrand, *Bibliographie Hellénique du XVII Siècle*, Vol. IV, pp. 252-254.

(13) Papadopoulos, *Cyril Lucaris*, pp. 29-30.

(14) Legrand, *op. cit.*, pp. 230-237.

(15) Hottinger, *Analecta Historico-Theologica*, p. 52 (1652).

(16) Simon, *The Critical History of the Religions and Customs of the Eastern Nations*, p. 47.

(17) Aymon, *op. cit.*, pp. 142-143.

(18) *Ibid.*, no date, pp. 172-175.

(19) *Ibid.*, no date, pp. 175-176.

(20) *Ibid.*, no date, pp. 193-195.

(21) *Ibid.*, no date, pp. 181-182.

(22) *Ibid.*, pp. 182-183.

(23) Legrand, *op. cit.*, pp. 329-340.

(24) Aymon, *op. cit.*, p. 164.

(25) *Ibid.*; see his letter to Uytenbogaert of October 10, 1613, pp. 130-164, and the one to De Wilhem, no date, pp. 177-179.

(26) *Ibid.*, pp. 183-184.

(27) *Ibid.*; see his letter of March 20, 1618, pp. 188-192.

(28) *Ibid.*; see his letter to Uytenbogaert, October 10, 1613, pp. 137-142.

(29) Papadopoulos, *op. cit.*, p. 36.

(30) Le Quien, *Oriens Christianus*, Vol. I, p. 331.

(31) J. Mihalcescu, "Les idées Calvinistes du Patriarch Cyrille Lucaris," in *Révue d' Histoire et de Philosophie Religieuse*, pp. 508-509 (1931).

(32) *Ibid.*; Leo Allatius, *De Ecclesiae Occidentalis et Orientalis Perpetua Consensione*, Liber III, pp. 1073-1074, Rome, 1655.

(33) Legrand, *op. cit.*, pp. 279-280.

(34) P. Colomesii, *Clarorum Virorum Epistolae Singulares*, pp. 557-559.

(35) *Ibid.*, pp. 559-561.

(36) See F. H. Marshall, "An Eastern Patriarch's Education in England," in *Journal of Hellenic Studies*, Vol. XLVI, pp. 191-192 (1926).

CHAPTER 6

ON THE ECUMENICAL THRONE

(1) Legrand, *Bibliographie Hellénique du XVII Siècle*, Vol. IV, pp. 340-342.

(2) See Cyprius, Χρονικὸν τῆς Ἑλληνικῆς Ἐκκλησίας, Vol. I, pp. 17-20, Franquerae, 1679; Smith, *Collectanea*, p. 22; Le Quien, *Oriens Christianus*, Vol. I, pp. 331-332.

(3) Allatius, *De Ecclesiae Occidentalis et Orientalis Perpetua Consensione*, Liber III, pp. 1074-1075.

(4) Aymon, *Monumens Authentiques de la Religion de Grèce*. Letter to Uytenbogaert, October 10, 1613, p. 161.

(5) M. Crusius, *Turcograecia*, Liber II, pp. 107-108.

(6) Paul Ricaut, *The Present State of the Greek and Armenian Churches*, pp. 95-97, London, 1679.

(7) Crusius, *op. cit.*, pp. 124-125.

(8) G. Finlay, *History of Greece*, Vol. V, pp. 47-49.

(9) J. P. von Hammer, *Histoire de l'Empire Ottoman*, French translation by J. J. Hellert, Vol. VIII, p. 46.

(10) Von Ranke, *History of the Ottoman Empire in the 16th and 17th Centuries*, p. 17.

(11) Finlay, *op. cit.*, p. 49.

(12) Crusius, *op. cit.*, pp. 126-127.

(13) Ricaut, *op. cit.*, p. 107.

(14) Pitton de Tournefort, *Relation d'un Voyage du Levant, 1700*, Vol. I, p. 118, Lyons, 1727.

(15) Aymon, *op. cit.*, p. 61.

(16) *Ibid.*, p. 65.

(17) Christophorus Angelus, *Status et Ritus Ecclesiae Graecae*, pp. 12-14, Francofurti, 1655; Von Ranke, *History of the Ottoman Empire*, pp. 6-21 *passim;* Finlay, *op. cit.*, pp. 39-41.

(18) De Tournefort, *op. cit.*, p. 123.

(19) *Ibid.*, p. 137.

(20) *Ibid.*, p. 84.

(21) Lest, however, we think too hard of the superstition of the old priest, we may remember our enlightened modern British-Israelites and the measurements of the Great Pyramid.

(22) Collison-Morley, *Italy after the Renaissance*, pp. 120-121.

(23) Ogg, *Europe in the 17th Century*, pp. 91, 343-344.

(24) Chrysoscule Logothetis, "Narration Historique des Troubles, que les Jésuites Suscitèrent à Constantinople," in Aymon, *op. cit.*, pp. 203-204. See also "Narratio Epistolica Turbarum inter Cyrillum Patriarcham Constantinoplitanum et Jesuitas," in Smith, *Collectanea*, pp. 85-86; P. Zottos, "Les Jésuites à Constantinople," in *Union Chrétienne*, p. 85 (1868).

(25) G. N. Clark, *The Seventeenth Century*, p. 302.

(26) A. J. Grant, *A History of Europe from 1494 to 1610*, p. 284. See also Collison-Morley, *op. cit.*, p. 121; Johnson, *Europe in the 16th Century*, p. 265; Griesinger, *The Jesuits*, pp. 48-52, 147, 265; Von Ranke, *History of the Popes*, pp. 172-173, 415-416.

(27) Aymon, *op. cit.*, p. 161.

(28) *Ibid.*, pp. 44-48; Colomesii, *Clarorum Virorum Epistolae Singulares*, p. 346.

(29) Allatius, *op. cit.*, p. 1069.

(30) As quoted by Zottos, *op. cit.*, p. 86; see also Logothetis, *op cit.*, pp. 202-204.

(31) See Von Hammer, *op. cit.*, pp. 165-166.

(32) J. T. Brent, *Introduction* to the volume published by the Hakluyt Society, Preface, p. iv (1893); M. A. Rambaud, in Lavisse et Rambaud, *Histoire Générale*, Vol. IV, p. 738.

(33) Lavisse et Rambaud, *op. cit.*, Vol. V, p. 877.

(34) Sandys, *Relation of a Journey Begun An. Dom. 1610*, p. 115.

(35) See Von Hammer, *op. cit.*, Vol. VII, pp. 140-141.

(36) Grant, *op. cit.*, p. 226.

(37) Von Hammer, *op. cit.*, Vol. VII, pp. 251-252.

(38) Lavisse et Rambaud, *op. cit.*, pp. 879-880.

(39) Sandys, *op. cit.*, p. 85.

(40) Baudier, *Inventaire de l'Histoire Générale des Turcs*, p. 761; Von Hammer, *op. cit.*, Vol. VIII, p. 192.

(41) J. B. Perkins, *Richelieu*, p. 165.

(42) Von Ranke, *History of the Popes*, Vol. II, pp. 242-244.

(43) L. F. von Pastor, *History of the Popes*, Vol. XXVIII, pp. 67-68.

CHAPTER 7

BEGINNING OF TROUBLE

(1) Logothetis, "Narration Historique des Troubles que les Jésuites Suscitèrent à Constantinople," in Aymon, *Monumens Authentiques de la Religion de Grèce*, p. 204.

(2) Leger, "Fragmentum Vitae," in Smith, *Collectanea*, p. 80.

(3) Cyprius, Χρονικὸν τῆς Ἑλληνικῆς Ἐκκλησίας, pp. 17-20.

(4) Simon, *The Critical History of the Religions and Customs of the Eastern Nations*, Vol. I, p. 332.

(5) Le Quien, *Oriens Christianus*, pp. 48-49.

(6) Hofmann, S. J., in *Orientalia Christiana*, No. 52, p. 46, May 1929.

(7) Logothetis, *op. cit.*, p. 204.

(8) Alphonse Guepin, *Un Apôtre de l'Union des Eglises au XVII Siècle*, p. 347, Paris, 1897.

(9) Allatius, *De Ecclesiae Occidentalis et Orientalis Perpetua Consensione*, pp. 985-989; Von Ranke, *History of the Popes in the 16th and 17th Centuries*, Vol. I, pp. 322-323, 433; Von Pastor, *History of the Popes*, Vol. XIX, pp. 239 ff.; Kidd, *The Counter-Reformation*, p. 180.

(10) A. Diamantopoulos, *Cyril Lucaris*, p. 37.

(11) Allatius, *op. cit.*, p. 989.

(12) *Ibid.*, pp. 1074-1075.

(13) As quoted in Von Hammer, *Histoire de l'Empire Ottoman*, Vol. VII, p. 345.

(14) Simon, *op. cit.*, pp. 48-49.

(15) Papadopolus, *Historia Gymnasii Patavini*, Vol. II, p. 294.

(16) Smith, *op. cit.*, p. 25.

(17) Logothetis, *op. cit.*, p. 205; "Narratio Epistolica Turbarum," in Smith, *op. cit.*, p. 87.

(18) In Smith, *op. cit.*, p. 81.

(19) Von Hammer, *op. cit.*, pp. 273-321.

(20) *Ibid.*, Vol. VII, pp. 362-363, Vol. VIII, pp. 16-17, 168-202.

(21) *Ibid.*, Vol. IX, p. 33.

(22) See Leger and Smith in *Collectanea, op. cit.*, pp. 26, 81.

(23) Sandys, *Relation of a Journey Begun. An. Dom. 1610*, pp. 90-92 *passim*.

(24) Logothetis, *op. cit.*, p. 207.

(25) Allatius, *op. cit.*, p. 1069.

(26) See Smith, *op. cit.*, p. 27; Cyprius, *op. cit.*, p. 19 says "menses tres."

(27) Smith, *op. cit.*, p. 27.

(28) Logothetis, *op. cit.*, p. 206; Smith, *op. cit.*, p. 88.

(29) Logothetis, *op. cit.*, p. 206; Le Quien, *op. cit.*, Vol. I, p. 333; Smith, *op. cit.*, p. 30.

CHAPTER 8

ROMAN INVASION

(1) George Codinus, *De Officiis et Officialibus Curiae et Ecclesiae Constantinopolitanae*, edited by Jac. Goar, p. 421.

(2) Von Pastor, *History of the Popes*, Vol. XXVII, pp. 16-17, 129-143.

(3) *Ibid.*

(4) Smith, *Collectanea*, p. 31.

(5) Logothetis, in Aymon, *Monumens Authentiques de la Religion de Grèce*, p. 210.

(6) See Hofmann, *Orientalia Christiana*, No. 52, pp. 35-36, May 1929; also Von Pastor, *op. cit.*, Vol. XXIX, p. 229.

(7) Von Pastor, *op. cit.*, Vol. XXIX, p. 228.

(8) Legrand, *Bibliographie Hellénique du XVII Siècle*, p. 159; Andronicos C. Demetracopoulos, *Orthodox Greece*, pp. 149, 152; *De Vita et Scriptis Metrophani Critopuli*, pp. 15-16; Sathas, *Modern Greek Literature*, pp. 308-309.

(9) Evdoxiu de Hurmuzaki, *Documente Privitore la Istoria Romanilor*, p. 225.

(10) Von Pastor, *op. cit.*, Vol. XXIX, p. 228.

(11) As quoted by Hofmann, *op. cit.*, pp. 47-48, December 16, 1623 in "Lettere della Congregazione: Lettere Volgari," Vol. 3, 34r-34v.

(12) Logothetis, in Aymon, *op. cit.*, p. 209; Smith, *op. cit.*, p. 31.

(13) Von Hammer, *Histoire de l'Empire Ottoman*, Vol. VII, pp. 185-189, Vol. VIII, pp. 147, 206, 217-218, 249, etc.

(14) *Ibid.*, Vol. IX, pp. 28, 54-56.

(15) Smith, *op. cit.*, p. 31.

(16) *Ibid.*

(17) For the instructions which were given to Cannachio Rossi, see Thomas Roe, *Negotiations in my Embassy to the Ottoman Porte, 1621-1628*, pp. 470 ff., London, 1740; Logothetis, *op. cit.*, pp. 211-214; Smith, *op. cit.*, p. 32.

(18) Smith, *op. cit.*, p. 32; Logothetis, *op. cit.*, p. 214.

(19) Demetracopoulos, *De Vita et Scriptis Metrophani Critopuli*, p. 9.

(20) Sathas, *op. cit.*, pp. 250-260; Demetracopoulos, *Orthodox Greece*, pp. 157-158; Papadopolus, *Historia Gymnasii Patavini*, Vol. II, pp. 298-299. This last writer gives by mistake to Corydalleus as his Christian name not Theophilus, but Nicephorus.

CHAPTER 9

THE CONGREGATIO IN RAGE

(1) Von Pastor, *History of the Popes,* Vol. XXVIII, pp. 1, 34-35; Collison-Morley, *Italy after the Renaissance,* p. 183.

(2) Collison-Morley, *op. cit.,* p. 139.

(3) *Ibid.,* p. 138; Ogg, *Europe in the 17th Century,* p. 400.

(4) Von Ranke, *History of the Popes,* Vol. II, p. 268; Von Pastor, *op. cit.,* p. 48.

(5) Von Ranke, *op cit.,* p. 320; Ogg, *op. cit.,* p. 402.

(6) Chasles, *Galileo Galilei,* p. 6.

(7) Von Pastor, *op. cit.,* pp. 30, 32.

(8) A. Leman, *Urbain VIII et la Rivalité de la France et de la Maison d'Autriche de 1631 à 1635,* pp. 245-247.

(9) Hofmann, *Orientalia Christiana,* pp. 36-37.

(10) Von Pastor, *op. cit.,* p. 5.

(11) *Scritture Riferite,* Vol. 270: 208v-209r.

(12) Von Pastor, *op. cit.,* Vol. XXIX, pp. 228-233.

(13) The book that the "Congregatio" had in mind was most probably a Greek translation of Bellarmin's *Christian Doctrine* which was prepared not by Eudaemon, but by Leonard Philaras and was published in 1616. Eudaemon audited the correctness of the translation. Legrand, *Bibliographie Hellénique du XVII Siècle,* Vol. I, pp. 105 ff.

(14) Legrand, *op. cit.,* p. 285.

(15) De Hurmuzaki, *Documente Privitore la Istoria Romanilor,* Vol. I, pp. 206, 208.

(16) Von Pastor, *op. cit.,* p. 233.

(17) Hofmann, *op. cit.,* pp. 36-37.

(18) Von Hammer, *Histoire de l'Empire Ottoman,* Vol. IX, pp. 29-30; Miller, *Essays* on the Latin Orient, p. 193; Ricaut, *Histoire de l'Empire Ottoman,* p. 30; Finlay, *History of Greece,* pp. 90-91, 100; Dallam, *The Diary of Master Thomas Dallam, 1599-1600,* pp. 17-18, 96-97.

(19) Vertot, *Histoire de Chevaliers de St. Jean de Jérusalem,* Vol. IV, p. 145.

(20) Smith, *Collectanea,* p. 33.

(21) Allatius, *De Ecclesiae Occidentalis et Orientalis Perpetua Consensione,* p. 1072; see also Logothetis, in Aymon, *Monumens Authentiques,* p. 215; Smith, *op. cit.,* pp. 33-35; "Narratio Turbarum," in Smith, *op. cit.,* pp. 98-99; Thomas Roe, *Relation of the Practices of the Jesuits Against Cyrillus Patriarch of Constantinople,* p. 758.

(22) Logothetis, *loc. cit.*

(23) Marquis de Bounac, *Mémoire Historique sur l'Ambassade de France,* pp. 10-14.

CHAPTER 10

THE PRINTING HOUSE IN CONSTANTINOPLE

(1) For the setting up of the printing house and its sequel see Smith, *Collectanea,* pp. 35-42; Leger, "Fragmentum Vitae," in Smith, *op. cit.,* pp.

77-83; Logothetis, "Narration Historique des Troubles que les Jésuites Suscitèrent à Constantinople," in Aymon, *Monumens Authentiques*, pp. 217-234; Allatius, *De Ecclesiae Occidentalis et Orientalis Perpetua Consensione*, Liber III, p. 1072; Hofmann, *Orientalia Christiana*, pp. 21-25, see also letter of De Cesy to Bethune of April 27, 1628, pp. 67-69.

(2) Logothetis, *op. cit.*, p. 218.

(3) Von Pastor, *History of the Popes*, Vol. XXIX, p. 216.

(4) Legrand, *Bibliographie Hellénique du XVII Siècle*, Vol. I, pp. 240-243.

(5) Mentioned by Legrand, *op. cit.*, p. 267.

(6) *Ibid.*, pp. 267-268.

(7) Logothetis, *op. cit.*, p. 221.

(8) Zinkeisen, *Histoire de l'Empire Ottoman*, Vol. IV, p. 374.

(9) Logothetis, *op. cit.*, pp. 229-234; Archives of Venice, as quoted by Von Hammer, *Histoire de l'Empire Ottoman*, Vol. IX, pp. 112-113; Letter of De Cesy in *Scritture Riferite*, Vol. 270: 176r-180v; Von Pastor, *op. cit.*, p. 233.

(10) Roe, *Relation of the Practices of the Jesuits Against Cyrillus Patriarch of Constantinople*, p. 742; Von Hammer, *op. cit.*, pp. 112-113.

(11) Von Hammer, *op. cit.*, pp. 114-115.

(12) Zottos, "Les Jésuites à Constantinople pendant le XVII Siècle," in *Union Chrétienne*, p. 95 (1868).

(13) Logothetis, *op. cit.*, p. 234.

(14) Dositheus, *History of the Patriarchs of Jerusalem*, Liber XI, p. 1174.

(15) Legrand, *op. cit.*, p. 243.

(16) *Scritture Riferite*, Vol. 270, pp. 210r-212r.

(17) G. J. Arvanitides, *Cyril Lucaris*, p. 107.

(18) Von Ranke, *History of the Popes in the 16th and 17th Centuries*, Vol. II, p. 280.

(19) Aldous Huxley, *The Grey Eminence*, pp. 104-113 *passim*.

(20) *Scritture Riferite*, Vol. 270: 212r-213r.

(21) Von Pastor, *op. cit.*, pp. 233-237.

CHAPTER 11

CONFESSIO FIDEI

(1) Legrand, *Bibliographie Hellénique du XVII Siècle*, Vol. IV, letter of February 8, 1628, pp. 353-354.

(2) *Ibid.*, pp. 352-353. See Minutes of the meeting.

(3) *Ibid.*, letter of March 12, 1628, pp. 357-358.

(4) *Ibid.*, letter of March 15, 1628, pp. 360-361.

(5) *Ibid.*, letters of March 24, 1628, pp. 361-365.

(6) *Ibid.*, minutes of meeting of June 2, 1628, pp. 368-369.

(7) *Ibid.*, letter of Leger to the Company, October 13, 1628, pp. 377-379.

(8) Smith, *Collectanea*, pp. 42-43.

(9) Legrand, *op. cit.*, letter of March 21, 1629, pp. 380-382.

(10) Cyprius, Χρονικὸν τῆς Ἑλληνικῆς Ἐκκλησίας, p. 188.

(11) Smith, *op. cit.*, pp. 71-73.

(12) In Mansi, *Sacrorum Conciliorum Nova et Amplissima Collectio* 34, pp. 1709-1720.

(13) In *Revista Teologica*, Jassy.

(14) In Mansi, *loc. cit.*

(15) *Ibid.*, pp. 1651-1775.

(16) Dositheus, *History of the Patriarchs of Jerusalem*, p. 1170, Bucharest, 1715.

(17) A. Diomedes Kyriakos, *Church History*, Vol. III, p. 327.

(18) M. Gedeon, *Lists of the Patriarchs*, p. 554.

(19) Papadopoulos, *Cyril Lucaris*, p. 105.

(20) A. Diamantopoulos, *Cyril Lucaris the Cretan*, p. 53.

(21) Sathas, *Modern Greek Literature*, p. 244.

(22) E. Velanidiotes, *Cyril Lucaris*, p. 62.

(23) C. Paparighopoulos, *History of the Greek Nation*, Vol. V, p. 68.

(24) J. Messoloras, *Symbolics of the Orthodox Eastern Church*, Vol. VII, Appendix A.

(25) Demetracopoulos, *National Almanac*, edited by M. P. Vrettos, pp. 41-51 (1870).

(26) Ch. Androutsos, *An Essay on Symbolics*, p. 33.

(27) D. S. Balanos, *The Confession of Cyril Lucaris*, p. 5.

(28) M. Renieris, *Cyril Lucaris, the Ecumenical Patriarch*.

(29) B. Georgiades, *Ecclesiastical Truth*, Vol. V, issue 7.

(30) Mentioned by Balanos in *The Lucarian Confession*, p. 4.

(31) J. Carmiris, *Orthodoxy and Protestantism*, Vol. I, pp. 211-213.

(32) Aymon, *Monumens Authentiques*, pp. 27-36.

(33) Legrand, *op. cit.*, pp. 400-406.

(34) *Ibid.*, pp. 473-474.

(35) *Ibid.*, pp. 329-340.

(36) *Ibid.*, p. 334.

(37) *Ibid.*, pp. 292-312.

(38) *Ibid.*, pp. 478-479.

(39) *Ibid.*, pp. 486-488.

(40) *Ibid.*, pp. 329-340.

(41) Hugo Grotius, *Votum pro Pace Ecclesiastica*, p. 57.

(42) A. Arnauld, *La Perpétuité de la Foi de l'Eglise Catholique*, Vol. VIII, pp. 543, 545.

(43) *Ibid.*, p. 544.

(44) Arvanitides, *Cyril Lucaris*, pp. 101, 119, 127.

(45) Diamantopoulos, *op. cit.*, p. 54.

(46) E. J. Kimmel, *Monumenta Fidei Ecclesiae Orientalis*, Vol. II, p. 1.

(47) *Ibid.*, Vol. I, p. 56.

(48) Schaff, *Creeds of the Greek and Latin Churches*.

(49) Hamilcar Alivizatos, *The Ministry and the Sacraments*, p. 68.

(50) J. Carmiris, *Metrophanes Critopoulos*, p. 170.

(51) Renieris, *op. cit.*, p. 54.

(52) Balanos, *op. cit.*, p. 11.

CHAPTER 12

NEW STORMS

(1) Von Pastor, *History of the Popes*, Vol. XXIX, p. 237.

(2) *Ibid.*, p. 238.

(3) Von Ranke, *History of the Popes in the 16th and 17th Centuries*, Vol. II, pp. 47-48, 97.

(4) *Ibid.*, Vol. I, p. 64.

(5) A. O. Legge, *The Growth of the Temporal Power of the Papacy*, p. 133.

(6) De Hurmuzaki, *Documente Privitore la Istoria Romanilor*, Vol. IV, Part I, pp. 682-683.

(7) Von Hammer, *Histoire de l'Empire Ottoman*, Vol. IX, p. 282.

(8) Smith, *Collectanea*, pp. 54-55 ;"Lettre du Sieur von Haghe," in Smith, *op. cit.*, pp. 73-74; Le Quien, *Oriens Christianus*, Vol. II, pp. 304-305.

(9) National Library of Paris, No. 16155-16195.

(10) Neale, *A History of the Holy Eastern Church*, Vol. II, p. 438.

(11) Hofmann, *Orientalia Christiana*, No. 52, pp. 99-100.

(12) Aymon, *Monumens Authentiques*, p. 102; Allatius, *De Ecclesiae Occidentalis et Orientalis Perpetua Consensione*, Liber III, p. 1077.

(13) Smith, *op. cit.*, pp. 56-57; Semnoz, "Les Dernières Années de Cyrille Lucar," in *Echos d'Orient*, Vol. VI, p. 101.

(14) Smith, *op. cit.*, p. 57.

(15) De Hurmuzaki, *op. cit.*, pp. 685-686.

(16) Von Pastor, *op. cit.*, p. 237.

(17) Von Hammer, *op. cit.*, p. 209.

(18) Aymon, *op. cit.*, p. 102; Smith, *op. cit.*, p. 55; Le Quien, *op. cit.*, p. 333.

(19) Le Quien, *op. cit.*, Vol. I, p. 334.

(20) Smith, *op. cit.*, p. 56.

(21) *Ibid.*

(22) *Ibid.*, p. 56; Le Quien, *op. cit.*, p. 334.

(23) Aymon, *op. cit.*, pp. 56-57.

(24) Smith, *op. cit.*, p. 56.

(25) Aymon, *op. cit.*, pp. 100-102.

(26) Hofmann, *op. cit.*, p. 33.

CHAPTER 13

THE TWO CYRILS

(1) Smith, *Collectanea*, p. 56.

(2) Le Quien, *Oriens Christianus*, Vol. I, p. 334.

(3) Hofmann, *Orientalia Christiana*, No. 52, p. 33.

(4) Smith, *op. cit.*, p. 56.

(5) *Ibid.*, p. 57.

(6) In Aymon, *Monumens Authentiques*, pp. 66-68.

(7) De Hurmuzaki, *Documente Privitore la Istoria Romanilor*, pp. 683-684.

(8) Smith, *op. cit.*, pp. 57-58.

(9) In Aymon, *op. cit.*, letter of April 26, 1635, pp. 77-78.

(10) *Ibid.*, letter of July 15, 1635, pp. 100-102.

(11) *Ibid.*, letter of April 26, 1635, pp. 77-78.

(12) *Ibid.*, letter of July 16, 1635, pp. 100-102.

(13) *Ibid.*, letter of April 4, 1635, pp. 66-68.

(14) *Ibid.*, letter of June 25, 1635, pp. 85-87.

(15) In Legrand, *Bibliographie Hellénique du XVII Siècle*, Vol. IV, letter of January 12, 1637, p. 493.

(16) Smith, *op. cit.*, p. 57.

(17) De Hurmuzaki, *op. cit.*, p. 684.

(18) Hofmann, *op. cit.*, p. 33.

(19) A. Papadopoulos-Kerameus, *Analekta*, Vol. IV, pp. 98-99.

(20) Legrand, *op. cit.*, p. 450.

(21) *Ibid.*, p. 493.

(22) Smith, *op. cit.*, p. 58; Le Quien, *op. cit.*, p. 334.

(23) Legrand, *op. cit.*, p. 450.

(24) Le Quien, *op. cit.*, p. 334.

(25) Gedeon, *Lists of the Patriarchs*, p. 561. The exact date of Cyril's return to the See is not well established.

(26) Le Quien, *op. cit.*, p. 334.

(27) Legrand, *op. cit.*, pp. 458-459.

(28) *Ibid.*, p. 461.

(29) *Ibid.*, p. 498.

CHAPTER 14

CYRIL LUCARIS—THE MAN

(1) From a letter of Rudolph Schmidt Schwarzenhorn we learn that Cyril had some correspondence with the King Gustavus Adolphus of Sweden; this fact explains the presence of his picture in Stockholm. (See De Hurmuzaki, *Documente Privitore la Istoria Romanilor*, Vol. IV, p. 682; Semnoz in *Echos d' Orient*, Vol. VI, p. 101.)

(2) Aymon, *Monumens Authentiques*, p. 158.

(3) *Ibid.*, pp. 100-102.

(4) *Ibid.*, letter to Leger of June 25, 1635, pp. 85-87.

(5) *Ibid.*, letter to Leger of March 10, 1637, pp. 115-119.

(6) Smith, *Collectanea*, p. 56.

(7) Aymon, *op. cit.*, letter of October 10, 1613, p. 135.

(8) *Ibid.*, pp. 134-135.

(9) *Ibid.*, undated letter, pp. 172-175.

(10) *Ibid.*, letter of May 30, 1619, pp. 183-184.

(11) *Ibid.*, undated letter, pp. 172-175.

(12) *Ibid.*, pp. 85-87.

(13) *Ibid.*, p. 136.

(14) *Ibid.*, p. 127.

CHAPTER 15

THE MARTYRDOM

(1) Aymon, *Monumens Authentiques*, pp. 77-78, 100-102.

(2) Smith, *Collectanea*, p. 59.

(3) Arvanitides, *Cyril Lucaris*, pp. 143-147.

(4) Semnoz, "Les Dernières Années de Cyrille Lucar," in *Echos d' Orient*, Vol. VI, p. 103.

(5) De Hurmuzaki, *Documente Privitore la Istoria Romanilor*, Vol. IV, p. 632.

(6) Smith, *op. cit.*, pp. 59-60. See also in Legrand, *Bibliographie Hellénique du XVII Siècle*, Vol. IV, pp. 457-458, a letter of Lucaris himself to the Pastors in Geneva, dated August 7, 1636 in which he states that in order to secure his last exile to Rhodes, his enemies had to wait until the Sultan departed to Asia Minor.

(7) Lavisse et Rambaud, *Histoire Générale*, Vol. V, p. 874.

(8) Von Hammer, *Histoire de l'Empire Ottoman*, Vol. IX, p. 311.

(9) *Ibid.*, pp. 315-316; see also Ricaut, *Histoire de l'Empire Ottoman*, Vol. I, pp. 139, 143.

(10) Smith, *op. cit.*, p. 59.

(11) De Hurmuzaki, *op. cit.*, pp. 685-686.

(12) Ricaut, *op. cit.*, pp. 119-120.

(13) Smith, *op. cit.*, p. 60; Legrand, *op. cit.*, Conopius' letter to Leger of July 4, 1638, pp. 514-516; Ricaut, *op. cit.*, p. 58.

(14) Von Hammer, *op. cit.*, p. 5.

(15) Lavisse et Rambaud, *op. cit.*, p. 852.

(16) Ogg, *Europe in the 17th Century*, p. 475.

(17) Von Ranke, *History of the Ottoman Empire in the 16th and 17th Centuries*, p. 25.

(18) Lavisse et Rambaud, *op. cit.*, pp. 852-853.

(19) Von Ranke, *op. cit.*, p. 25; see also De Tournefort, *Relation d'un Voyage du Levant*, 1700, Vol. II, p. 287.

(20) Von Hammer, *op. cit.*, p. 306.

(21) Smith, *op. cit.*, pp. 60-61.

(22) Hottinger, *Analecta Historico-Theologica*, Zurich, 1652, pp. 564-566.

(23) Allatius, *De Ecclesiae Occidentalis et Orientalis Perpetua Consensione*, Vol. III, p. 1075.

(24) Hofmann, *Orientalia Christiana*, p. 107.

(25) Smith, *op. cit.*, p. 61.

(26) Pococke, in his Supplement to the *Historiae Dynastiarum*, gives the date as January 27, 1638, but as he informed Smith, "January" was a misprint for "June."

(27) In the details of Cyril's death, the author follows chiefly the account of Conopius given in his letter to Leger of July 4, 1638, in Legrand, *op. cit.*, pp. 514-516. See also Papadopolus, *Historia Gymnasii Patavini*, Vol. II, p. 294; Le Quien, *Oriens Christianus*, Vol. I, pp. 334-335; Allatius, *op. cit.*, p. 1075; De la Croix, *Etat Présent des Nations et Eglises Grecque, Arménienne et Maronite en Turquie*, 1715, pp. 5-7.

(28) Hofmann, *op. cit.*, p. 107.

(29) De Hurmuzaki, *op. cit.*, pp. 685-686.

(30) See Schwarzenhorn's report, De Hurmuzaki, *op. cit.*, p. 689; Semnoz, *op. cit.*, p. 106; Gedeon, *Lists of the Patriarchs*, p. 568.

(31) Smith, *op. cit.*, p. 62.

CHAPTER 16

ACHIEVEMENTS AND ASSESSMENTS

(1) Legrand, *Bibliographie Hellénique du XVII Siècle*, Vol. IV, encyclical letter of March 4, 1636, pp. 432-448.

(2) Simon, *Critical History of the Religions and Customs of the Eastern Nations*, p. 183.

(3) Legrand, *op. cit.*, pp. 504-506.

(4) John Evelyn, *The Diary of John Evelyn, F. R. S.*, edited by William Bray, p. 7. See also Henry Savage, *Balliofergus, or a Commentary on the Foundation of Balliol College*, p. 121 (1668), and Anthony Wood, *Athenae Oxonienses*, Vol. II, col. 1140 (1721).

(5) *Album Studiosorum Academiae Lugduno Bataviae*, col. 359, La Haye, 1875.

(6) Allatius, *De Ecclesiae Occidentalis et Orientalis Perpetua Consensione*, Vol. III, pp. 1020-1021; Simon, *op. cit.*, p. 52.

(7) Demetracopoulos, *Corrections to Sathas' Modern Greek Literature*, p. 68.

(8) The author failed to discover a copy of that book or a description of it in any of the authorities on Greek literature of the 17th century.

(9) Smith, *Collectanea*, p. 62.

(10) Legrand, *op. cit.*, pp. 486-488.

(11) Ricaut, *The Present State of the Greek and Armenian Churches*, pp. 15-16, London, 1679.

(12) Von Ranke, *History of the Popes in the 16th and 17th Centuries*, Vol. I, pp. 64-66.

(13) R. B. Lloyd, *The Approach to the Reformation*, p. 176.

(14) J. Mackinnon, *The Origins of the Reformation*, p. 417.

(15) *Ibid.*, pp. 128-139 *passim*.

(16) T. M. Lindsay, *History of the Reformation*, Vol. I, pp. 117-118.